Acknowledgements

Sincere thanks are due, in particular, to my clients for their talent, creativity and willingness to take a risk with their presentations. They were the inspiration for this book.

My special thanks go to my daughter Polly Sampson for her interest and practical help. My thanks too to my partner, Alan Felton, an ace presenter, for his encouragement and support.

First published in Great Britain and the United States in 2003 by Kogan Page Limited

120 Pentonville Road
London N1 9JN
UK
www.kogan-page.co.uk

22883 Quicksilver Drive
Sterling VA 20166-2012
USA

© Eleri Sampson, 2003

ISBN 0 7494 3853 3

British Library Cataloguing-in-Publication Data

A CIP record for this book is available from the British Library.

Library of Congress Cataloging-in-Publication Data

Sampson, Eleri, 1944-
    Creative business presentations / Eleri Sampson.
        p. cm.
Includes bibliographical references and index.
    ISBN 0-7494-3853-3
    1. Business presentations. I. Title.
    HF5718.22.S26 2003
    651.7'3--dc21

                                                                2002154868

Typeset by Jean Cussons Typesetting, Diss, Norfolk
Printed and bound in Great Britain by Biddles Ltd, Guildford and King's Lynn
www.biddles.co.uk

Contents

iv   Contents

Introduction

The better we can communicate as human beings, the better we will do our jobs and the better we will do business with each other. Setting about the process of being a better presenter means starting off on a journey to learn about how to present your authentic self to the world, to harness your emotions, your senses and your instincts to your intellectual, logical self.

My aims are as follows:

- To make this book an easy read, so that you can dip into it at random and find something interesting, amusing or challenging wherever you open it. You don't have to work from the introduction straight through to the back cover if you don't want to; you can browse from the back to the front and cherry-pick anything that attracts your attention.

- To provide clues for the clueless, instant inspiration for the eager, easy-to-copy ideas for the experienced but weary presenter, and impetus for the unimaginative so that you can generate your own ideas.

- To stress the importance of supporting verbal messages with visual imagery by the use of pictures, cartoons, diagrams, activities, questionnaires, bulleted lists etc to support the text so as to appeal to those of you who don't learn by reading.

- To include some background material by way of explanation if you prefer models and theories on which to build your understanding.

This book is not intended as an academic work; it is a pragmatic approach to using the whole brain, acknowledging the power of multi-intelligences and encouraging you to get in touch in with your senses. I'm not going to focus on the 'hard' skills of making a presentation – stuff to do with structure, content and how to use equipment – although these are very important and are dealt with. Instead, I'm going to focus on the 'soft' skills – style, emotion and imagination.

My key objective is to provide you with tips and techniques to help you enhance your professional impact through your natural style as a presenter with ideas for creative approaches giving you the 'soft skills' to support the 'hard skills' of delivering a presentation. I can't guarantee it will work. However, I can guarantee it won't work if you don't try it.

PART I

Presentation essentials

1 'Natural' presentations

Searching for a way to bring some lightness and freshness to a 'Brush Up Your Presentation Skills' workshop for senior executives, I wondered what would perk them up and capture their attention. I knew that they were all experienced presenters, but some had become jaded, some had lost their confidence because of a bad experience and others were just tired. My instinct told me they were ready to 'play' – provided that they had a guarantee that they would go away with something that would quickly improve their public persona through presenting more effectively.

They already had 'hard' presentation and media skills born of many training courses and solid experience. What was missing was the 'soft' skills, the emotional, creative, colourful skills that were going to make them fall in love with presenting again and make their audiences fall in love with them. I came up with the idea of using a whole brain approach that I knew about from recent developments in classroom teaching techniques. Whole brain learning involves combining left brain activities such as logic, structure, data and rules with right brain activities such as having fun, discussing, asking questions, playing and experimenting – so-called natural learning. Eureka! A perfect match. We called it the LUDIC workshop (from the Latin *ludere* – to play).

We asked each other what exactly is being tested when you are invited to make a presentation? We came to the conclusion that it is a test of personal style more than of knowledge (unless you are a specialist) and also about how you:

- organize your information;
- explain complex issues.

Moreover, it tests:

- your level of confidence/timidity;
- your ability to hold an audience;
- your level of authority;
- your credibility;
- your skill at handling questions.

It is useful to remember that what is *not* usually being tested is your knowledge of the subject. You wouldn't have been asked if there was a question mark around your knowledge. I shall presume that you wouldn't be stupid enough to present unfamiliar or unresearched material.

As a result of this experience, and my work with individual clients, I come to you as a tribune for the Natural Presentation Style Party. Working with both accomplished and novice presenters, I have come to realize that all that soul-searching about how to give a cracking presentation boils down to a handful of truths. I have identified seven; please add any of your own. Rather like stars, they are quite random but brilliant when seen together.

1. It's OK to be yourself.

2. 2 or 3 key points are all you need

3. Your audience is not the enemy

4. You don't have to be perfect to be successful

5. Humour helps

6. You can't avoid preparation

7. Take a whole brain approach

THE PRESENTATION PRESCRIPTION

1. It's OK to be yourself

There's no such thing as a perfect presenter. If you can stand up with confidence, speak clearly, gain the audience's attention and deliver your message with style and clarity and without relying on a battery of technology, you are, or at least will look like, a natural presenter. A natural style, like a 'natural' face, requires both art and artifice as well as honesty, as anyone who wears make-up will know.

'Where is there dignity unless there is honesty?'
(Marcus Tullius Cicero, philosopher, 106–43 BC)

2. Two or three key points are all you need

You don't need yards of facts and shedloads of clever phrases. You need two or three key points that you are utterly familiar with and can talk about with ease. If you have to make a long or complex presentation, are running a workshop or giving a seminar, then you give your audience the details in the form of notes and break down the whole presentation into bite-sized pieces, each of which only needs two or three key points.

There is a delicious irony to this tale of a 'Brush Up Your Presentation Skills' workshop, in Sheffield. While on the train going there, and in the process of getting my material and overheads in order, I noticed that although I had printed out the overheads I had neglected to print out the accompanying notes. A good opportunity to remind myself firmly that if you know what you're talking about, you only ever need two or key points.

3. Your audience is not the enemy

If you find giving a business presentation stressful, then you are the enemy, not your audience. There is no evidence except experience for the 80/20 factor, and I believe in it utterly. In a presentation context it breaks down like this:

20% of the audience will either adore you or hate you and your presentation;

80% of the audience will find you and your presentation perfectly OK.

Of that 20 per cent, 5 per cent will dislike you and your presentation and 15 per cent will be mad about you and your presentation.

4. You don't have to be perfect to be successful

Learning from failure is a hard lesson for some of us. This message is for perfectionists everywhere. If your performance is not 'perfect' in your eyes, you are liable to see yourself as a total failure. This leads to your becoming a victim of all-or-nothing negative self-talk, which in turn leads to despondency and stress. Stop it! Stress commonly arises from our striving to meet an ideal. Ideals are just that, not reality.

> **'If you want to increase your success rate, double your failure rate.'**
>
> *(Thomas Watson, founder of IBM)*

5. Humour helps

Whatever your style, whatever the presentation topic and whatever the audience, all except the most solemn occasions are enhanced by a bit of humour. You're not expected to be a stand-up comedian, just to adopt a light touch. When people laugh, they relax, and that's how you want them.

> **'What are the essential ingredients that make a brilliant speaker?**
>
> **An ability to be completely spontaneous on stage. To be able to interact with the audience. To be a good communicator who can deliver high-quality content in a passionate way. And to make people laugh.'**
>
> *(Brendan Barnes, Speakers for Business)*

6. You can't avoid preparation

Even the most elegant, relaxed, apparently spontaneous speakers have spent time in preparation, planning and rehearsal. They make it look easy but they most certainly will have spent time formally or informally, in their heads or in real time, gathering data and rehearsing how they will use it. Martin Luther King's widow said that her husband spent many hours in their kitchen perfecting one of the most powerful and natural-sounding speeches of all time.

> **'A true circus artist will not make a single unconsidered movement in the ring.'**
>
> *(Nell Stroud, who ran away to join the circus, from Josser: The secret life of a circus girl, Virago, 1999)*

7. Take a whole brain approach

Put simply, our brains are composed of two distinct hemispheres that are connected in the middle by a bundle of nervous fibres called the corpus callosum. The logic or linear hemisphere – the left one – deals with the parts, the details, the processes of language and linear analysis. The global or gestalt hemisphere – the right one – deals with the processing of wholes, with images, emotion and intuition. We all exhibit a preference for one side or the other but it is necessary to use both hemispheres to be proficient at anything – making a presentation is an obvious example.

THE FOUR CORNERSTONES

There are also a handful of absolute basics: four cornerstones on which a presentation is built. The four cornerstones are:

- being able to cope with your nerves;
- being able to make a presentation interesting for any audience;
- being able to build rapport;
- being able to handle questions with confidence.

Coping with nerves	**Creating interest**
Building rapport with the audience	**Handling questions with confidence**

THE FOUR CORNERSTONES SELF-CHECKER

You might find it useful to make a note as you go of any 'aha' moments.

Where did I start from on this topic?

'...need all the help I can get'; '... just need a bit of a brush-up.'

What's become clear to me?

Why is it meaningful for me?

What tip have I picked up?

How can I brand it with my personal style?

When can I try it out?

THE MAGIC CARPET

One of the techniques used very successfully in coaching is finding a metaphor for a situation or dilemma. This technique is incredibly effective when working on presentation issues, particularly those to do with confidence. Having pondered on the notion of seven presentation rules, people find their own metaphor or visual symbol for how they can carry their invisible support system with them. The originality that flows from people who swear they have no imagination is marvellous. Some examples:

'Seven keys attached to my belt.'

'Seven stars that shine above my head.'

'Seven sisters standing in solidarity behind me.'

'Seven jewels set in a ring that I wear on my little finger.'

'An avenue of tall poplar trees, strong and rooted, in a line before me.'

'Invisible scaffolding that I climb up on.'

'An invisible bumbag round my waist that holds all my positive thoughts and experiences that no one can steal.'

My favourite is an image of a magic carpet. One that 'takes me wherever I want to be and has the seven presentation precepts woven into the pattern. I stand on it and I am my best self.'

KEY WORDS

Creative

According to the *Concise Oxford Dictionary*, 'creative' means *inventive and imaginative.*

- inventive: *original in devising, showing ingenuity of devising*
- imagination: *1. a mental faculty forming images or concepts of external objects not present to the senses; 2. the ability of the mind to be creative and resourceful*
- ingenuity: *skill in devising or contriving*
- original: *1. existing from the beginning; innate; 2. novel, inventive, creative; 3. serving as a pattern; not derivative or imitative*
- originality: *newness or freshness*

One of the most terrifying sights for a writer, painter or designer is a blank sheet of paper. Being creative doesn't have to mean starting from nothing. Being creative can also mean knowing a good idea when you see one, being given half an idea and providing the other half or a better one, getting a glimpse of an idea and looking out and about making connections, finding patterns and raising possibilities for developing ideas.

Business

According to the *Concise Oxford Dictionary*, 'business' means 1. *engaged in trade or commerce; 2. one's regular occupation, profession or trade.* Business is about creating a market, buying and selling ideas, goods and services.

We all do deals during our working and non-working life. Sometimes we want to sell, sometimes we want to buy.

Presentation

According to the *Concise Oxford Dictionary*, 'presentation' means 1 *a demonstration or display of materials, information etc: a lecture; 2 an exhibition or theatrical performance.* So much business is transacted via 'presentations':

- management consultants pitching to a prospective client;
- manufacturers positioning a new product;
- candidates for a job presenting their ideas to a an interview panel;
- speakers at a conference sharing the latest thinking with their colleagues;
- team leaders enthusing about new ways and new strategies to their team;
- the board of a company reporting to a shareholders' meeting;
- directors reporting to the board.

A presentation is not a lecture. It doesn't need the density of information that characterizes a typical academic lecture and it doesn't require the formal structure of a speech, neither is it as informal as a talk. So, a presentation can mean one person or a team of people sharing ideas, facts, information, opinions with a group of other people – anything from a conference of thousands to a meeting of two or three people. Thus it can take in team briefings, committee meetings, sales pitches, board meetings, public meetings, seminars, workshops, job interviews, media interviews and press conferences.

There is a difference between a 'presentation' and a 'speech', a 'lecture' and a 'talk':

- A 'speech' is a formal, public address such as might be delivered by a politician or a bride's father.
- A 'lecture' is a discourse giving information about a subject to a class or other audience, in which the lecturer speaks or writes learnedly and at length.
- A 'talk' is informal.

What they have in common is that they all have an audience and that they could all benefit from creative treatment.

CREATIVITY

How many of the statements are true for you? The traits indicated in these statements are commonly found in creative people. The more YESs you scored, the more creative you are likely to be. The more NOs you scored, the less creative you are likely to be. If you would like to take a more creative approach to making business presentations, then why not shift a gear? Just one shift in attitude, one small change of behaviour, can make a world of difference.

Table 1.1   Are you a creative personality?

	Yes	No	A bit
I am an independent self-starter.			
I have a degree of non-conformity.			
I get absorbed in my work.			
I am persistent.			
I can tolerate ambiguity.			
I am determined.			
I am intuitive.			
I have a well-developed aesthetic sense.			
I am a risk taker.			
I am not frightened of the possibility of failure.			
TOTALS			

DIGITAL THINKING

Digital thinking is not a sense but a brain function and is a very common way of thinking and behaving and presenting material. Many of us think this is our preferred style because it is how we were taught at school, but it may or may not be our best style. You can be competent in this area but have no passion. You can also be pretty useless in the digital realm and feel a failure unless you have been rewarded for another type of intelligence. Digital or logical thinking is a form of imageless thinking that we often come across in mathematicians and scientists, and is concerned with facts and data.

How many of these statements are true for you? The traits indicated in these statements are commonly found in digital personalities. The more

YESs you scored, the more digital you are likely to be. The more NOs you scored, the less digital you are likely to be. If you would like to take a more creative approach to making business presentations, then why not shift a gear? Just one shift in attitude, one small change of behaviour, can make a world of difference.

Table 1.2   Are you a digital personality?

	Yes	No	A bit
I like playing games such as chess that require logical thinking.			
I like to experiment with things to see how they work			
I like to group or categorize things in order to understand their meaning and relevance			
I prefer to take a systematic, step-by-step approach to problem solving.			
I can quickly find logical flaws in someone else's behaviour or opinions.			
I find it easy to do the household accounts and balance a chequebook.			
I like to prepare detailed lists and checkpoints for business and at home.			
I readily analyse arguments and situations.			
I am interested in maths, science and technical developments.			
TOTALS			

LEARNING TO BE MORE CREATIVE

Learning to be more creative means that you can entertain and engage your audience and get your message across more effectively by using interesting, unexpected or original ways and means. Being more creative or imaginative doesn't have to mean being wacky, anarchic or embarrassing – although it can if you want it to. It's more to do with adopting symbolism, making associations, using your imagination, exaggerating, having fun, looking for other ways, shifting your thinking. Being creative is about 95 per cent perspiration and 5 per cent inspiration. When designing, planning and eventually delivering a presentation, a presenter, like an artist or designer, should always have the discipline, structure and skills of his or her craft to rely on when inspiration fails.

> **'If people are to work with paint, clay or fiber, they must learn how to use tools, how to make what they have conceived, how to temper creativity by patience. It is this last capacity which is perhaps the most difficult and most important to cultivate. Craftsmanship requires the ability to keep the pulse of creativity beating slowly over long periods of time.'**
> (Sir Misha Black, Crafts magazine, 1976)

Shift a gear

- Ask, 'What if?', 'Why?' and 'Why not?'
- Take a different perspective. Stop looking in the same old places.
- Don't accept the first idea you get.
- Look outside your own interests and specialisms.
- Challenge assumptions.
- Daydream.
- Walk a mile in someone else's shoes.

Shift your attitude

- Be open to new experiences.
- Welcome change.
- Don't be discouraged by setbacks or failures.
- Stop being a perfectionist.
- Be less dependent on the familiar.
- Remember that experiments can fail.

Shift your behaviour

- Don't always wait for instructions or approval before you act.
- Consider breaking some rules.
- Consider not bowing to social pressure.
- Develop more self-sufficiency.

WHY BOTHER TO MAKE YOUR BUSINESS PRESENTATIONS MORE CREATIVE?

If you make your business presentations more creative, it will:

- help you to gain more visibility;
- help you to be more influential;
- give you a more recognizable personal style;
- help you to reach more of the people more of the time.

Being a player in today's business world is like playing 'total football'. By that I mean that you have to play all your talent, all the time, because you are constantly on show, being assessed and appraised by customers, clients, colleagues and competitors alike. Delivering an effective and memorable presentation is one of the key challenges in business life today. The ability to speak well on your feet, along with time management, financial awareness and people management skills, should be just another tool in your business skills toolbox.

Speaking well in public is also a key to leadership. The degree to which you communicate effectively in public will determine how seriously people will take your ideas and whether they will be prepared to follow your lead.

MORE ABOUT 'YOU DON'T HAVE TO BE PERFECT TO BE SUCCESSFUL'

The by-product of working with clients on their presentations, trying to get inside their heads to understand what is blocking them, is that I gain insights into ways of improving my own performance. One insight, painfully gained over the years, is that there is no such thing as a 'perfect presenter'. I tried to understand what made good presenters good and realized that they communicate with everything they have. They create rapport with their audience. They reach parts of the audience other presenters cannot reach because they communicate with their heart and soul, mind, body and emotions. They engage all of their audience's senses – they show pictures, tell stories, ask questions, reveal something about their private selves and personal opinions, interact with their audience and make them feel, touch and taste their message.

MORE ABOUT TAKING A WHOLE BRAIN APPROACH

When you want your presentation to be more effective – to be more memorable and engaging – there are three simple rules:

1. Use right and left brain.
2. Reach more than one type of intelligence.
3. Access the senses.

1. Use the whole brain

Get the right brain and left brain to work together. Harness imagination to intellect, daydreaming to reality. For an audience to lock something into their memory you will need to use emotion as well as intellect; humour, fun, passion as well as logic and numbers; non-verbal as well as verbal communication; colour as well as black and white. Some people like to take in information in a slow, step-by-step fashion – the linear learners. Others need to have an overview, to see the big picture – the global learners. Accessing and using both the linear and global style, *flexing* your own style, is a whole brain approach.

> **'We buy on emotion – justify with facts.'**
> *(Bert Decker, US communication expert)*

2. Reach more than one type of intelligence

Recent academic research has identified 10 or more intelligences. The theory of multiple intelligences (MI) has been developed by the psychologist and Harvard theorist Howard Gardner and challenges old beliefs about what it means to be intelligent. Gardner believes that our culture places too much emphasis, both within and outside our education systems, on verbal ability and logical thinking and in so doing has neglected other ways of knowing, other abilities and talents. We have come to realize that typical intelligence tests only predict success in language, logic and maths and are useless predictors of possible success in the real world as indicators of artistic, business, social or creative abilities.

How many ways can you be intelligent? At least 10 ways, maybe more:

- linguistic;
- digital/logical/mathematical;
- visual (visuo-spatial);
- kinetic;
- musical;
- interpersonal;
- intrapersonal;
- naturalist;
- emotional;
- spiritual/existential.

Although you may identify strongly with only one or two of the descriptions of intelligence, you, along with all other human beings, possess all of the intelligences. However, it's a rare individual who reaches a high level of competence in every one.

I have grouped intelligences into four creative preferences for this book:

- sound;

- movement;
- language;
- pictures.

3. Access the senses

A sensory experience is a physical one. We use our senses in different proportions to collect and assess data. People are able to recall:

20% of what they read
30% of what they hear
40% of what they see
50% of what they say
60% of what they do
90% of what they see, hear, say and do

It follows that your presentation should attempt to reach your audience using a combination of seeing, hearing, saying and doing.

'Leaving the arts to one side for a moment, it seems particularly strange that we are having to struggle for creativity generally in schools, across all subjects, when we have a world which is increasingly recognised as crying out for innovation in every conceivable activity... Safety within parameters, made familiar by the tickboxing and form-filling of our time, shields potential rebels from the thrills of making unlikely connections, thinking beyond the obvious and generally taking intellectual risks.'
(Michaela Crimmin, Head of Arts, Royal Society of Arts, Journal, 2 June 2001)

2   Your style

The heart of a good presentation is YOU, the presenter, and your style: who you are, how you are and what you know – the power triangle of personality, behaviour and knowledge.

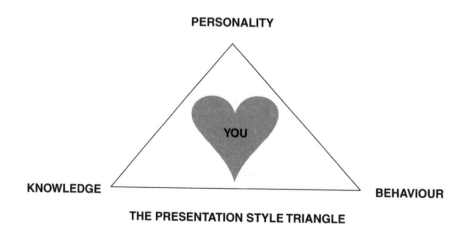

PERSONALITY

YOU

KNOWLEDGE

BEHAVIOUR

THE PRESENTATION STYLE TRIANGLE

Most people think of making a presentation as simply talking. But talking is only a part of it. Making a presentation involves not only what you say but also how you say it, and takes into account the way you look, your body language, your use of space, your charisma and public persona. You don't have to change *who* you are to be a more creative presenter; just change, temporarily, *how* you are.

PRESENTATION STYLE – NATURE OR NURTURE?

People are always looking for keys to help them unlock their understanding of themselves and others and to be better at what they do. They want to attack this problem in practical ways that are easy to understand and fast to achieve, so incorporating some 'style sorting' into presentation skills development makes sense.

The concept of personality types has been around for a long time and behavioural psychologists agree that communication styles fall into broad groupings. Similarities occur across much research and from many test instruments. My favourites are, first, MBTI® (Myers–Briggs Type Indicator), which sorts people into 16 personality types, and second, 'My BEST Communication Style', which sorts people into four communication styles. Both are based on established and respected principles and have maintained their usefulness and validity over the decades, and I value their integrity and accuracy.

MBTI®

The Myers–Briggs Type Indicator is one of most respected psychometric instruments in the world. It has been around since 1962 and its purpose is to make the theory of Carl Jung's psychological types understandable and useful in people's lives. For me, its strength as an aid to understanding yourself and your audience is that it is not about assessing your skills, ability or intelligence. It *sorts* rather than *judges*. The essence of the theory is that seemingly random behaviour is actually quite orderly, owing to the differences in the way people prefer to 1) use their perception – about things, people, happenings and ideas, and 2) use their judgement about ways of coming to conclusions about what has been perceived.

When you take the Indicator, the four preferences that you identify as being the most like you are combined into a four-letter personality type that you will recognize if you've been 'done' – for example, ESFJ or INTP. There are 16 personality types. All preferences are regarded as equally valid, important and valuable. The MBTI is a self-reporting instrument that looks at eight possible preferences, organized into four bi-polar scales:

Extraversion	E	I	Introversion
Sensing	S	N	Intuition
Thinking	T	F	Feeling
Judging	J	P	Perceiving

All types exist, although not in equal numbers, and in any audience there will be a mixture of types, so it makes sense to design a presentation that has a good chance of communicating across all types, not just the types similar yourself. However, some communication clashes are inevitable if you take into account the spread of types within the population. For example, according to Isabel Myers, *Estimates of Type Distributions*, Consulting Psychologists Press (1962):

● About 75% of the population in the United States prefer E (Extraversion).

- About 75% of the population in the United States prefer S (Sensing).
- About 60% of males in the United States prefer T (Thinking).
- About 65% of females in the United States prefer F (Feeling).
- About 55–60% of the population in the United States prefer J (Judging).

Big picture or detail?

The preferences for gathering evidence are S (Sensing) and N (Intuition). The S/N scale is probably the most useful to consider when preparing material for a business presentation – how you are going to manage the information in terms of big picture or detail. Do you focus on facts or possibilities? Or both?

Consider these options for starting a presentation:

1. Start with the big picture and move on to the details.
2. Start with the details and work up to the big picture.
3. Start with the big picture and stay with the big picture.
4. Start with the details and stay with the details.

Try to assess what approach your audience is likely to prefer, by either inclination or occupation. There's a chance that analysts or accountants would prefer option 4 and that entrepreneurs would prefer option 3. But this is to risk stereotyping, so if you don't know and are unable to find out, or realize that it's going to be a very mixed group, then it would be sensible to flex your style to include other preferences. When in doubt, go for option 1.

Try this test:

How many 'F's are there in the box below?

> **THE FEDERAL FUSES ARE THE RESULT OF SCIENTIFIC RESEARCH COMBINED WITH THE FRUITS OF EXPERIENCE.**

What was your chosen problem-solving process?

- Read it all first then went back and counted.
- Intuitively, scanned the whole sentence and guessed.
- Worked letter by letter, line by line.
- Read and listened to the sounds in your head.
- Read out loud and listened to the sounds.
- Counted backwards, ignoring the sense of the words.
- Some other way.

'MY BEST COMMUNICATION STYLE'

My BEST Communication Style, by James H Brewer (1989), is based on the work of Myers and Briggs and sorts communication styles into four groups.

Typical characteristics of each of the four styles are shown in Table 2.1.

NATURAL OR ADOPTED STYLE?

Your natural style can be your greatest strength; however, you may discover that it has been layered over with formal techniques, bad

Table 2.1   Brewer's classification of communication styles

Bold (B)	Expressive (E)	Sympathetic (S)	Technical (T)
Will take charge	Entertaining	Dependable	Good planner and researcher
Can inspire	Spontaneous	Reliable	Enjoys details
Is brave	Can lift the mood	Persistent	Accurate, will double-check facts and figures
Will achieve objectives	Will seize unexpected opportunities	Laid-back	Thorough
Get results	Persuasive	Doesn't panic	Serious about quality

habits or lack of confidence and that your natural, most effective style is hidden or submerged. I encourage people to discover their natural style and work on the strengths of that style rather than try to 'cure' or disguise the weaknesses of their adopted style. Most people have one dominant natural style supported by a second. Some people have a blend across one or more styles. There is no one style that exclusively gets results, although there are, of course, basic communication techniques that will always work.

Three quick ways to hit the target are:

● language, vocabulary
● body language
● vocal pace

	1. Language	2. Body language	3. Vocal pace
Bs	Direct	Movement	Fast
Es	Inspirational	Movement	Fast
Ss	Emotional	Stillness	Slow
Ts	Factual	Stillness	Slow

THE PORRIDGE PRINCIPLE OF EFFECTIVE PRESENTATION

We all know the story of 'Goldilocks and the Three Bears' – how Goldilocks visited the house of the three bears and tried out the beds, the furniture and the porridge to establish if they were right for her. She wondered whether they were 'too hot, too cold, or just right'. Like Goldilocks, we could take a glance at our presentation style and enquire whether our style is 'just right'.

P	Prepared	Not over-prepared, or carelessly unprepared, everything checked against the plan
O	Organized	Well-organized but not obsessive
R	Ready	Not over-anxious or too confident, mind and body ready for take-off
R	Rehearsed	Not over-rehearsed, or under-rehearsed but relaxed and familiar with the material
I	Interactive	Not emptily performing, but engaging on a human level with the audience
D	Delighted	Not too laid back, keen but not manic
G	Grounded	Being in the moment, not wishing it over or worrying about previous experiences
E	Energetic	Not too bouncy, not too flat

HUMOUR

You're not expected to be a stand-up comedian, but whatever your style, humour helps. All except the most solemn presentations are enhanced by a light touch. Especially appealing are stories against yourself. Self-deprecating humour is universally charming. Who can you think of who uses humour successfully in their presentations? Ask them what it feels like to make an audience laugh. How do they do it?

'My responsibility is to train young actors in comic character. The central thing is what we call Clown, or finding your comic persona. If you imagine there's a big part of most of us that's a complete idiot, and we spend all our time trying to hide that,

what I do at the start of the Clown course is try to find it... and from there we begin to see where they might form a character and what type of idiot they might be.'

> (Mark Bell, actor and movement instructor at the London Academy of Music and Dramatic Art, whose speciality is teaching students how to create comic characters, talking to Candida Crewe in the Times on Saturday, 2002)

PRESENTATIONS – PLEASURE OR PAIN?

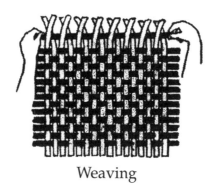

Weaving

'Without the warp there can be no weft, for woven cloth is built on the warp: until the weft interweaves with the warp there can be no cloth.'

> (Bernat Klein, textile designer, b 1922)

A piece of intricately woven cloth is a neat metaphor for personality and behaviour:

● **warp:** the downward anchoring threads – the basics, the givens, and our genetic inheritance stretching from birth to death;

- **weft:** the threads going across – what we put in, and the accidents of life, what happens to us: 'the interplay of planning, chance and circumstance'.

The warp and weft of your life will produce your behaviour. Your presentation style is part of your behaviour and a product of personality and experience, nature and nurture. When we are under slight stress, our authentic style surfaces. If, as psychologists tell us, personality is stable over time, it's reasonable to expect behaviour to be stable as well. However, we do behave in inconsistent ways, so we shouldn't expect to deliver the same kind of presentation every time. Your style may vary because of recent experiences, the way you feel, the current situation at home or at work, or a change in your role or status. It's useful to be aware of the style that seems to be your best fit, the one that seems most comfortable most of the time.

How you have arrived at your presentation style is a mixture of your past presentation history mixed with your personality type, your training and upbringing. How did you develop that style? Just suppose for a minute that you are a doctor, a GP meeting a patient for the first time. Having asked the patient the 'what seems to be the matter' question you take his or her medical history. Looking back helps you to discover past symptoms and illnesses, which together with the current symptoms help you to make a diagnosis and prescribe the appropriate treatment.

Now imagine you are a presentation skills doctor. Like a medical doctor, the first thing you would do is to take the patient's presentation history by asking two kinds of questions: 1) objective questions about the event, the circumstances, the audience, what you did; and 2) subjective questions about how you felt. Why not be your own doctor and ask yourself these questions and see if you can come up with a diagnosis and a course of treatment?

BE YOUR OWN PRESENTATION SKILLS DOCTOR	
Objective questions	**Your responses**
1. When did you last do a presentation?	
2. Where did it take place?	
3. Who was there?	
4. What was it about?	
5. How many times before have you given this presentation?	
6. What evidence do you have of the success or otherwise of your performance?	
7. To what extent were your personal outcomes met?	
8. What was the main outcome?	
Subjective questions	**Your responses**
9. How did you feel – at the time? before? after?	
10. How did you do? What were your impressions?	
11. What feedback did you get?	
12. What went well?	
13. What went badly?	
14. What would you change?	
15. As a result of previous presentations, what have you learnt about – yourself, audiences, presentations?	
16. What would you like to work on in order to improve?	

Learn not to be disappointed when the audience doesn't love your style even when the content and technical delivery are brilliant. Make them admire your professionalism even if they don't respond to your charisma. Depending on your style and your message, you can come over well to one audience but not to another. A quick-witted, attention-grabbing presentation style will work for a big crowd but might be criticized round a serious meeting table. What is perceived by one audience to be entertaining and stimulating could be seen by another as marginal and frivolous.

> **'It was an unimpressive performance from the start: slouched, hand in pocket, he seemed not to care. He bumbled through key findings in what I'm sure he thought of as an informal manner. But informal can be code for unrehearsed and ill-thought-through. As he lost his audience he took refuge in statistics.'**
>
> *(Khalid Aziz, critiquing a business presentation in Management Today)*

Answer to the quiz: There are six 'F's. Did your method get you the correct answer?

3   Your audience

I must have done hundreds of presentations over the years, and which audiences do I remember? The rotten ratbags. I come home after a presentation and debrief. 'What were they like?' Alan always asks. My most vivid recollections involve:

- arrogant analysts;

- beastly barristers;
- horrid housemen.

I came across some research about interpersonal perception that put forward the notion that 5 per cent of people you meet in life won't like you. If that's the case, it's only reasonable to suppose that 5 per cent of your audience won't take to you no matter how knowledgeable or personable you are. Stop worrying about the 5 per cent and accept that the whole world won't love you. Alan and I give the worst audiences nicknames because naming them and making light of them eventually makes them seem less awful.

Most people would rather you, not they, were doing the presentation. If so few of my audiences were a trial to me, then 95 per cent must have been OK or even better than OK. Reframing the memory, I say, 'Awful audiences are great material for supper party conversations', and I remind myself of the rave reviews, the adventures I've had and the fascinating people I've met.

The audience members are never there by chance. They have a specific purpose in being there, as well as a set of expectations. The audience is never an empty vessel waiting to be filled. Its members come with their own sets of attitudes, opinions, prejudices, preconceptions, levels of education, life experiences, emotions, feelings and values. A new audience sees you out of context. Those present know that there is more to you than their immediate impression of you, but for the brief moment in time you and they are together, and because we are all busy people, NOW is the only reality. Find out what they want, give them respect and give them the best you've got.

This chapter is divided into three sections:

1. building an audience profile;

2. involving the audience;

3. handling questions.

Let's start by getting to know something about the audience.

WHAT ARE THEY LIKE? BUILDING AN AUDIENCE PROFILE

Collect whatever information you can by whatever means you can. Build the audience profile by collecting information about its size, composition, prior knowledge and propensity. If your topic was 'Business Planning for a Small Business' and if your audience was composed of childminders from an inner city on one occasion and free-lance accountants on another, then although the material might well be the same, the approach would be different. Useful information might include:

- age;
- economic status, salary range, having a mortgage or not, property owning or not;
- education;
- Emotional Quotient and Intelligence Quotient;
- expectations;
- gender;
- level of responsibility;
- marital status, number of children;
- overriding feelings (suspicion? fear? eagerness?);

- passions and drives;
- pet peeves;
- political persuasions;
- role and status within the organization;
- religious values.

One way to find out what the audience might be like if you don't know them is to work through a list of opposite characteristics:

hostile	friendly
decision makers	information seekers
want entertainment	expect a sales pitch
purely social	definitely business only
all specialists	general knowledge
all know each other	all strangers
high profile	low profile
small and friendly	large and impersonal

Another technique is to make a checklist. Keep a master copy with your presentation materials or design a template on your PC and make up a fresh one for each presentation:

- Who is going to be there? What are their names and job descriptions?
- How many of them will there be?
- What is their age range?
- Will there be both men and women?

- What is their level of seniority?
- What are their expectations?
- What specialist knowledge do they have?
- Do they want to be there?
- Do they have any prejudices?
- Do they have any strong religious or political beliefs?
- Why should they want to listen to me?
- Are they like me or not like me?

You can use this information to assess the situation and plan accordingly. When time is short, go over the audience profile and check three areas that will be the most significant, then build your presentation round one or all of those. For example:

- If they are specialists in the same subject as you, concentrate on getting your facts straight, but have something special up your sleeve: new information, surprising facts. Be ready to flatter them and ask them for their views.

- If it is a large and impersonal group who may not know each other, share a personal anecdote; be a bit larger than life; include the audience by asking rhetorical questions or posing imaginary problems for them to solve.

- If they have any prejudices, address them right up at the front of the presentation and get them out of the way. Don't let the audience bully you with their prejudices, but don't ignore them either.

Other ways to collect data

You could:

- Greet people individually when they enter a room. Shake hands, introduce yourself if necessary, find out a bit about them before you start. Remember their names to use in the course of your presentation.

- Treat everyone you meet as if he or she is the most important person you will meet that day and show that you respect his or her needs.

- Phone up one in ten of the audience and find out what they really want to get out of your session.

- Send out a pre-course questionnaire.

- Get a detailed brief from the most senior person involved.

INVOLVING THE AUDIENCE

'The great thing about being famous is that you can bore them and they think it's their fault.'

(Henry Kissinger)

Making your presentation interesting is one of the cornerstones of presenting. Some of the audience will always have part of their mind or feelings involved with something else: their internal emotions or some external event. You may not know about their feelings but you can acknowledge external or corporate events.

- If there has been an international or national event of great importance or a local incident that is consuming people's hearts or minds, give them the opportunity to share how they feel or describe what's happened to them. Decide on a time limit. Let them get it off their chest to the whole group or to a neighbour. Refocus and begin again.

● Depending on the strength of interest in the room, you could include an update slide in your PowerPoint presentation or write a note on the flip chart following a break:

– Sports results: tennis, golf, football, athletics, round-the-world yacht race and so on. The information is particularly easy to access if the company is a sponsor of the sport.

– Oscar winners.

– Lottery winning numbers.

– Breaking news, such as election results.

– Hot gossip about celebrities, or departmental or corporate gossip.

Two-day events are tiring for everyone, but my co-presenter and I weren't prepared for one of our attendees to fall asleep. It wasn't even after lunch. We were aware that she had dozed off and we were all rather embarrassed. We didn't know if we were being boring or if she wasn't well or had had a bad night. We managed to get through the session without waking her up even though we resorted to dropping heavy objects, moving around the room and asking the group questions. How silly of us not to have openly acknowledged the situation and called a break.

Ask the audience...

● ... **to answer a question.** They can call out the answer, share it with a neighbour, keep it in their heads or write it down.

- – 'How do you feel right now?' Ask your audience to respond by using descriptive alliterative word pairs, eg Tired Tessa, Enthusiastic Eric.
- – 'Who is the most respected person in your company today?'
- – 'What is the exchange rate for the Canadian dollar today?'

● **... to divide into groups.** They can discuss topics from one of your key points.

● **... for a volunteer.** This immediately gets their attention. You can feel the buzz as the keen ones hope they'll get picked and the shy ones pray they will magically acquire Harry Potter's invisibility cloak.

● **... to ask questions or make observations.** Invite the audience to divide into small groups to discuss an issue you've raised or to formulate questions or observations to share with you and the rest of the audience.

● **... to vote on something.** They could put their hands up, or do it Roman style: thumbs up, thumbs down, or flat palm wiggle to signify so-so.

● **... to write on the flip chart.** Ask someone from the audience to write on the flip chart instead of doing it yourself.

Tape something under their chairs

Questions in sealed envelopes, a number or a coin; the audience has to look for them at a given moment.

Award a prize

A book, your book, booklet, bar of chocolate.

Give something away

Give away a copy of a book or booklet you've written, an appropriate CD, an audio cassette of hints and tips, the address of an interesting or useful Web site.

Invite your audience to use their imagination

'I'd like you to imagine a situation in the future when everyone works from home' or 'How would you feel if your team were relocated to Sydney, Australia?'

Design a PING (Packet Internet Groper, from a computer networking technique)

To 'ping' means to get someone's attention, to send out a signal to see which of an organization's computers are present, switched on and paying attention.

Give them a pencil and paper task to perform

The following are some suggestions:

- Acrostic – ask the audience to devise a poem or other composition in which certain letters in each line form a word or words.

- Anagram – invite the audience to unravel an anagram, one of the key words or phrases from your presentation.

- Bingo – use key words from your presentation.

- Crossword puzzle – let the audience solve a puzzle in which the answers are key words and phrases that you will be using or have been using in your presentation.

- Quiz – find out how much they know or don't know abut your topic before and/or after you've done your slot.

Give them a physical activity to do

Ask them to put their hands up, stand up or sit down in answer to a question, eg 'How many people travelled here by car today? How many walked, cycled, came by train, tube?'

Use everyday objects

Incorporating everyday objects that people are likely to have on them can provide you with opportunities for some interaction with your audience. The trick is to find a connection between one of your points and the object in a way that doesn't appear contrived or silly. Or use this device to wake them up, challenge them or engage in a bit of impromptu rivalry. For example:

- Small change. Have you got a 50 pence coin? Don't look. How many sides does it have?

- Season ticket. When does it expire?
- Driving licence. When does it expire?
- Travel ticket. What are the dimensions of your ticket?
- Credit card. What is your account number?

How could you incorporate the following items into a presentation?

- tissues;
- hankie;
- glasses cleaning cloth;
- glasses;
- reading glasses;
- pen;
- pencil;
- earrings;
- ring;
- watch;
- necklace;
- notepad;
- contents of wallet;
- contents of purse;
- contents of cosmetic bag;
- hairbrush/comb;
- keys;

- mobile phone;
- notebook;
- palmtop;
- anything else.

HANDLING QUESTIONS

'If you lose your rag, you lose your audience!'
(Alan Felton, actor and lecturer)

Handling questions well is another cornerstone of presentations and is a good way to enhance your credibility, because this is where the audience test out what you really know and whether they should follow you. Maybe this is why some people in the audience seem to have a mission to discomfit you. It's as though they were genetically programmed to ask the most awkward question, to sit with a disapproving look glued to their faces, to interrupt, to be sarcastic or otherwise undermine your efforts. Maybe they're bored, attention-seeking, showing off their own knowledge or skills, or want to put you right on a matter of fact. Or they might set off on rambling observations unconnected to the topic, or want to put their own concerns on your agenda.

If they are irritating you, consider some tactics for dealing with them. They are always in a minority but seem more numerous than they really are. The simplest rules of engagement are:

- Don't retaliate.
- Don't argue.
- Stay polite.

- Don't panic.
- Ask them to repeat the question/criticism/objection.
- Don't make a promise you can't keep just to get out of the situation.

General tactics for handling questions

- If thinking on your feet is not one of your gifts, then try to anticipate what questions might be asked – what kind of questions are probable, possible or unlikely. Prepare answers to them all – the easy ones and the tough ones.

- State in your introduction how you would like to take questions. Taking questions as you go may slow things down and you may lose focus, but can make the presentation more interesting because you will keep your presentation audience-focused, addressing issues the audience really want to address. Taking questions at the end means you can control the timing and keep yourself focused.

- Listen carefully to the question – the actual words, the tone of voice and any underlying message. What kind of question is it?

  - Is it really an opinion disguised as a question?

  - Is it intended to test your knowledge?

  - Is it a real quest for information?

- Jot down key words while the questioner is speaking to help you frame your response.

- If appropriate, restate the question for other people in the audience who may not have heard it clearly.

- Answer briefly. It's not the time for a mini-presentation.

- If you don't know the answer to a question, give yourself time to think, then if you still don't know just say so; don't try to bluff your way out. You can always suggest you look up the answer later and meet the person afterwards or e-mail them.

● Suppose you gave out the wrong facts? In that case, admit you were wrong, thank the questioner for pointing it out and move on.

● If the questioner is aggressive, keep your cool. The audience will usually be on your side and will not support the questioner's behaviour. Indicate that you would be willing to meet them alone later! Just because they've asked the question doesn't mean you have to answer it.

Take the opportunity to shine

Some presenters sparkle at question time. They love the opportunity to think on their feet, to be tested, to be witty and quick, to show how knowledgeable they are or how human they are.

The audience is not the enemy

The conference was in the library of a management centre, very nicely set up for a series of speakers running through the day, with a long table for the chair and speakers. The table was covered in a baize cloth and had water glasses, a vase of flowers and so on. I wanted to rearrange the space for my session and moved this large glass vase of flowers from the table because it was obscuring my view of the audience. Unfortunately, the rim of the glass broke and I cut my hand quite badly. I was wearing a yellow jacket and I was more concerned about getting blood on it than how I was going to get on with my presentation. Fortunately there were two Directors of Nursing in the audience who between them sorted me out and applied first aid, and the show went on.

4   Your material

> *Security is being on the right side of the knowledge gap*

The more often you do something in the same way, the less easy it is to consider doing it another way. When you're preparing material for a presentation, if you get stuck or don't know where to start, do something differently. Give your routine a bit of a jounce, then be prepared for new ideas to follow. Wherever you start, when you are considering putting a presentation together, it would be as well to check some basics before you do too much preparation.

Cover the basics

- Do you have a clear and realistic purpose?
- Who will be your audience?
- How much time have you got?
- What is the main objective of the presentation?
- What topics will you be covering?
- What topics won't you be covering?
- Is your topic a suitable one for the medium of a live presentation?

What are your key objectives?

It helps if at an early stage you are clear about your key objectives, both overt and covert. What is your brief? What are your main messages? What outcome do you want to achieve?

Your overt objectives for the presentation might be:

- to sell a new idea;
- to share a strategy;
- to share data;
- to enthuse about changes;
- to explain new systems;
- to introduce procedures.

You can break down these large overt objectives into smaller sub-objectives, which in turn give you your main topic headings.

Your covert objectives for the presentation might include wanting to:

- show your colleagues you can deliver a polished presentation;
- prove to yourself that you can be articulate and persuasive;
- improve the way you manage your time in a presentation;
- try out some new material;
- experiment with ways of handling your nerves;
- build your confidence;
- increase your visibility;
- get some presentation practice;
- position yourself for promotion;
- be better known within your profession;
- influence the right people.

If you are clear about your key objectives and your main messages, you can make a start on your PPR routine: **Preparation – Planning – Rehearsal**:

Preparation	Planning	Rehearsal
1. Collect	1. Design a structure	1. Arguments for and against
2. Collate	2. Identify support material	2. Timing, talking to the clock
3. Edit	3. Make a map	3. Full dress rehearsal
4. Entrances and exits	4. 30 second message	

PREPARATION

1. Collect

Where do you start? You could try the Three-Step Preparation Process. This doesn't have to be a step-by-step activity if you are not a linear person. Good ideas might visit you at any stage; just be sure to catch them. You might feel more disciplined or more inspired on one day and not the next; you might do a brilliant job editing your material even if you haven't done all your research. You can jump in and out wherever you like, provided that you jump on every step.

Draw from a wide range of material for illustrations, anecdotes and examples; don't just centre on your topic. History, geography, politics, literature, sport and showbiz are all rich seams to plunder and sources of possible inspiration. How you collect your material will depend, like so many other aspects of presentation skills, on your personality. You may prefer to be orderly and systematic, collecting material, filing and indexing it for easy retrieval, allowing yourself loads of time. You may have a more chaotic approach, be pressure-prompted and work into the night when inspiration seizes you. You could start by collecting objects or images connected with your theme or its development and build the words round the images.

Whatever your style, you have to start somewhere. If you are a beginner or feel a bit jaded or out of practice, try any of these:

- Make a mind map – a non-linear approach using spider-like connections, coloured pens, drawings.
- Brainstorm, by yourself or with a team.
- Make lists.
- Open up named files on your PC to take the notes.

- Start a card index system.
- Utilize a box file for cuttings and images.
- Use one of the old-fashioned research methods:
    - a library visit for primary and secondary sources;
    - newspapers;
    - professional journals;
    - trade magazines;
    - periodicals.
- Use a variety of search engines, not the same old one.
- While on the Internet, use links to visit anything that looks promising.
- Jot down notes on Post-it notes and stick them on a board, wall, floor.
- Have a notebook by the bed, in the bathroom, on the desk or by the phone so you can record a brilliant notion when it visits you.
- Speak your ideas into a Dictaphone when in the car.
- Use your computer's voice recognition programme to dictate notes.
- Talk your ideas through with someone else and get them to make some notes and feed them back to you.
- Talk to people who are knowledgeable or who have controversial views on your topic to give you some impetus.
- Talk to people to test out your ideas and theories. Talking not only clarifies but can generate ideas too.
- Collect pictures, images, cartoons.

2. Collate

If you haven't already done it, this is the moment to clarify the title of your presentation and check that you have chosen the right subject. Avoid titles that are too general. The more specific the better, because this primes the audience about what to expect and what not to expect. For example, take 'Challenging Convention: Creativity and Cross-disciplinary Projects in Local Government'. Here, the key words are:

- challenging;
- convention;
- creativity;
- cross-disciplinary;
- local government.

These are your headings. All your other material flows from them.

Decide the order in which you will present your material. Group all the information you have collected under your key headings for your main messages. Then divide the material into key points and minor points. You might want to take the sensible and logical approach or the adventurous approach to collating material. Either way, you have to decide which are your two or three main messages.

Have an adventure, trust to chance

Throw all your material for any section in the air and see how it lands; it might give you fresh inspiration. Put it in alphabetical order and see what sort of flow that gives you. Order it by length instead of content. Challenge yourself to incorporate something you select randomly – for example, take a word from the dictionary or technical handbook. The '... and finally...' item on the TV news and the third leader in a broadsheet newspaper both provide a source of light but interesting material that you might be able to use.

Turn your title round to find out what the opposite could mean. Is that really what you're *not* going to talk about? Take the opposite view to the one you are presenting; does your story stack up?

Count the number of jargon words, technical terms, buzzwords or phrases you have used. What is the frequency of these in relation to the rest of the text? More than one in a hundred is too many. Try replacing these words with everyday language – does your piece seem better or worse? What's happened to the balance? Unless your audience is as used to the jargon as you are, steer clear of it.

3. Edit

All your material must get past your presentations bouncer whose job it is to let in only your key objectives and main messages; 'no trainers, no exceptions'. Your bouncer, like St Peter at Heaven's Gate, has some hard questions to ask you before your presentation will be able to pass through and gain entry:

- Does this piece of information meet your key objectives?
- Does this piece of information contribute to your minor objectives?
- Does this piece of research contribute to your main theme or any of the sub-themes?
- Does this example take your argument forward?
- Is this data essential, desirable or merely quite interesting?
- Have you fallen in love with this piece of information because it's so intriguing and you fought so hard and spent so long finding it?
- Are you willing to let this information go?

4. Entrances and exits

Be utterly familiar with your opening and closing remarks. There's no need to learn them parrot fashion; just be sure you can deliver them with authority, with your head up and making good eye contact.

PLANNING

1. Design a structure

Are your ideas usually in a big jumble, like utensils in the kitchen drawer, clothes dropped in a heap on the floor, crockery in confusion in a cupboard, or are they ordered in a logical and pleasing way? There is something very satisfying about a well-crafted presentation.

Simple structure

- Tell them what you're going to tell them.

- Tell them.

- Tell them what you've told them.

Classical structure: beginning, middle and end

Beginning:

- Introduce yourself (if necessary).

- Catch the audience's attention.

- Make your opening remarks.

- Set out the aim of the presentation, why the audience should listen to you.

- Introduce the topic areas and outline your presentation.

Middle

The middle is the body of the presentation. It is usually in three stages with a recap made of each stage before moving on to the next one.

Discuss the main ideas of your presentation, arranged in a logical way. There is more than one kind of logical progression that you can take to order your material:

- big picture to detail;
- cause and effect;
- chronological, in date or time order;
- detail to big picture;
- general to specific;
- geographic order;
- historical sequence;
- macro to micro;
- problem to solution;
- sequentially, step by step;
- small and familiar to large and less familiar;
- specific to general.

End

The end should comprise a summary or interpretation of your main points, putting your main points in perspective. Do not introduce any new material. Make your concluding remarks, thank the audience and ask for questions.

Back of an envelope structure

- An object or prop.
- Opening remarks that answer the question: WHY should I be talking to you?
- THREE
- KEY
- WORDS
- Close.

2. Identify support material

Your support material is crucial to the success of your presentation. Each of your key points and each of your minor or supporting points should be supported by illustrations, facts, evidence or research. If you make the way you expand and illustrate each point rather different each time, you will keep the audience's interest. Challenge yourself to ring the changes between anecdote and research evidence, cartoons and charts, and so on.

- Illustrate each point differently.
- Repeat the main message in different ways.
- Take an audience-centred approach.
- Make it interesting.

For ideas about selecting support material, see Chapter 5.

3. Make a map

People like to know where they're going and what they'll be doing on the way. Make sure that your planning includes a map for the audience. This could take the form of a slide showing the structure of your presentation. Let them know at the beginning what you will be covering, your intentions and the scope of the session, then offer signposts along the way. Why do you need a structure? To help the brain establish a pattern and create expectations. Your chosen structure is a way of ordering your material so that you know what is going to go where, and to help you to decide how you are going to illustrate each point.

4. Your 30-second message

I remember coming across a small yellow paperback at the bookshop on Paddington Station. The book was *How to Get Your Point Across in 30 Seconds – or Less* by Milo O Frank, a business communications consultant and film writer–producer who lives in Beverly Hills. He said something like this:

Thirty seconds may not seem like a long time. You can speak about a hundred words in that time. But it's long enough to gain your audience's attention, to persuade them, to challenge them, to make them laugh or see your point of view. Half a minute is the attention span of most human beings before their mind wanders off to sex or shopping or something else. Radio and television news programmes make use of the 30-second attention span when planning news stories and look for 'soundbites' of this length. The task is to convey the essential heart of your message in 30 seconds. This exercise will help you to stay focused, keep on track, and be more concise.

That was a 30-second message.

REHEARSAL

1. Arguments for and against having a rehearsal

The case against

Some very competent presenters don't rehearse. Well, they don't rehearse physically in the sense that they go over and over what they intend to do and say in advance of the performance. They do their own kind of rehearsal: thinking, planning and considering options and alternatives without actually staging a mock-up of a performance. This is usually because although they like to make themselves familiar with their material, they don't want to lose their spontaneity on the day. They feel that rehearsal or over-rehearsal will make them lose their 'edge'. This 'no rehearsal' method works for presenters who are fairly experienced, confident people; people who are familiar with their material and can cut and paste as the situation demands and who also, crucially, have a preference for a little risk taking.

> A risk-filled strategy, but a very successful one, was something I tried for the first time on a group of City law librarians. I gave everyone in the audience a small stack of Post-it notes and asked them to write down what they most wanted to find out. All the ideas were put up on a display board and I designed a structure before their eyes, grouping similar topics, discarding irrelevant ones and focusing on majority interests. Worked like a dream. You need heaps of confidence and a deep knowledge of the subject to make this approach fly.

The case for

Rehearsing the content, timing, props, costume and special effects of the presentation is what gives many presenters the confidence they need. Speaking the words, making the moves, acclimatizing themselves to the room and feeling the atmosphere contribute to their sense of control. The advantages of a rehearsal are to check on timing, spot things that might go wrong and help with fluency in the delivery of the script.

> '**I used to say that if I'd wanted to do presentations all day I'd have gone to drama school. Now I realize that being a competent presenter will get you noticed and get you where you want to be. I still don't relish doing presentations. Preparation is my bullet-proof vest!'**
>
> *(Polly Sampson, Manager)*

Timing, talking to the clock

You must know how much time you have been allocated for your presentation. You can't begin to structure the content until you know this – it influences your whole strategy. The worst sin of a presenter (apart from being boring) is to go on for too long. Going on past your allotted time is rude and inconsiderate. People have other things to do; other speakers may have to follow you. The audience won't thank you for it, the chairperson won't thank you for it and other contributors will certainly wish you off the podium. If you've ever had to follow someone who has over-run, you will know the anxiety and frustration it inspires as you try, mentally, to adjust your presentation to take up less time. Not everyone can do this, especially if they are prone to nerves or don't like to change their plans at short notice.

If you are a beginner, time your presentation and rehearse it carefully with and without notes. There is a tendency for people to waffle if they go off-script too much. If you are more experienced, always work with a clock in front of you and cut and paste as you go, according to how your material is going down. If the audience can see the clock as well, cover it with a piece of paper so that they can't count the minutes.

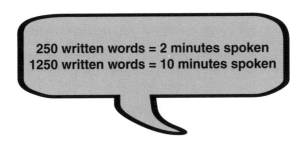

250 written words = 2 minutes spoken
1250 written words = 10 minutes spoken

3. The full dress rehearsal

You need an audience for the full dress rehearsal, as well as a mirror, a clock and a stiff drink or a cup of tea afterwards. Go through the whole presentation with all your props, script, support material and mock it up as realistically as you can. Your audience can consist of a mirror, video recorder, a friend, the cat. It doesn't matter so long as you make eye contact with them.

If you are given the opportunity to run through your presentation at the venue, then accept immediately if you can find the time, particularly if it's a big set-piece affair with a lot of staging and technology. Make friends with the technicians and they'll look after you. Give them a copy of your script even if you're not going to read from it; it will give them an idea of the structure of your presentation, however sketchy, and it should at least have a running order for slides, music or special effects.

Rehearsing in your head

When you are familiar with your material, you can go over it in your head. Rehearsing in your head strengthens the neural pathways. The brain stores a symbolic representation of the act or movement, so that when you come to do it for real, your brain knows you've done it before and makes it easier for you. Dancers, footballers, surgeons and public speakers regularly use this form of creative visualization.

Get in the mood

After a good rehearsal, get into presentation mood while you are on your way to the event, walking along a corridor, from car park to meeting room or from base to the event location. Be properly dressed en route; don't get changed in the car or in the cloakroon unless you absolutely have to.

Use everyone you meet on the way as an opportunity to project your best professional self. Your body language will exhibit positive signals all the way and so it will be easy to slip into presentation mode when you need to.

5 Your support material

You can move your presentation from a passive event to an engaging event the moment you support your spoken word with visuals and interactive moments. The job of your support material is to help you to make a connection with your audience, to enhance your key message and to make it memorable. Use fewer words and more graphics.

We know that in any group of people there will be a range of preferences for receiving and retaining information. We all have different learning styles, different intelligences and different sensory dominances. In your audience you will have individuals who are different in every way:

● different learning styles – the note taker, the doer, the reflector, the talker and so on;

● right or left brain dominance – logic or imagination, detail or big picture;

- different communication styles – direct or indirect, data focused or people focused, action orientated or value centred, and so on;
- sensory dominance – left- or right-handed, left- or right-footed, right or left eye dominance, left or right ear dominance;
- visual, auditory or kinaesthetic preferences.

VISUAL SUPPORT FOR YOUR MESSAGE

Use an overhead projector

Overheads are an excellent choice when you have a larger audience, say 25 or more. It makes sense to vary your slide design to take into account differences in perception. You could put some images on the right, some on the left, some centred. Have some slides with a picture, some with charts or diagrams, some with numbers, some with text, and some with a mixture of these.

Tips for new users

- Use a light background for overheads and a dark background for on-screen presentations and slides.

- You might want to include your name or the company logo and a page number on each slide.

- Take the backing sheet or the sticky alignment strip off each acetate before you start; it looks clumsy and is distracting to be stripping them off as you go.

- Look around for suitable images to create your own distinctive slides. Magazine cuttings, photographs as well as clip art will act as a resource.

- Turn the projector off when you change slides so that the light doesn't blind the audience. This doesn't apply if you are going to slide them across quickly and there are only half a dozen or so.

- Don't talk about a different subject to the one that is displayed on-screen.

- Turn the projector off if you intend to talk at length between slides; the motor is noisy and distracting.

At a corporate training event, the OHP platen wouldn't take the protective flaps of the acetate holder; every single acetate had to be taken out of its holder and placed on the platen. Nothing to be done in this case except 'just do it'.

A simple PowerPoint presentation about how to use the OHP:

USING THE OHP
5 basic rules

1. Preparation
- Ensure everyone can see the screen
- Check and clean equipment
- Arrange slides and materials
  - in order
  - within easy reach

2. Planning
- One idea per transparency
- Include only essential facts
- Be brief
- Be accurate

3. Design
- CAPITALS for TITLES or EMPHASIS
- **Bold for headings**
- Lower case letters
- Sans-serif font
- 30 characters per line
- 6–8 lines per transparency
- Align from the left

4. Use Display Techniques
- Overlay
- Slow reveal
- Mask
- Bullets
- Animation

5. Use Proper Presentation Technniques
- Avoid projecting your own shadow
- Don't look over your shoulder
- Point to the transparency not the screen
- Use a pointer not your finger
- Switch off between transparencies
- Switch off, to switch audience focus

The same presentation using a standard PowerPoint template (the original is in colour):

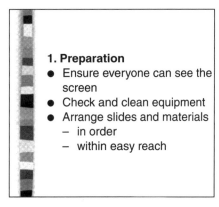

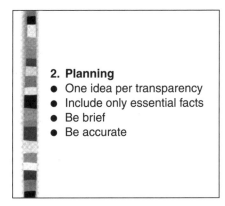

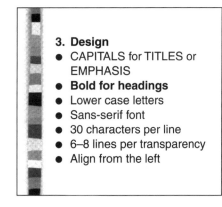

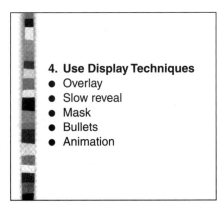

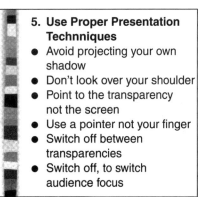

A presentation that uses a quotation and an image on each slide as a trigger for thoughts and emotions, rather than to deliver a factual message:

Career Development Workshop

Eleri Sampson
Sampson Rees Executive Coaching and Personal Development Programmes

---

"Looking in"
Career Anchors

"What holds you firmly grounded in life can also stop you from sailing away."

The Change Curve

CRISIS
Relief
Shock
Denial
Anger
Bargaining
Guilt
Panic
Depression

OPPORTUNITY
Building
Acceptance
Resignation

**Managing the Future
– an inside-out approach**

Looking in

Looking out

Looking around

"Looking out"
The Interview

"An interview is not an exam. There are no right answers, only appropriate responses."

Managing the Future

"We all have choices about how we behave. We can be passive, reactive or proactive in any situation."

Use 35 mm slides

My husband and I were invited to give a two-handed talk, supported by his pianist, to the members of a convent in Chelsea. I was to go first, to give an illustrated talk about Victorian costume, and Alan was to follow with Victorian songs and ballads, with Alison providing the accompaniment. We turned off the lights and I began. After the second slide there was a soft 'puff' sound from the projector and suddenly it was on fire. Someone in the audience had the presence of mind to switch off the power and the equipment was removed for examination. In the corner of the room was a blackboard and I found myself presenting in the old-fashioned 'chalk and talk' way, drawing on the blackboard the detailed construction of Victorian corsets, meanwhile sending up thanks for my pattern-cutting training. The smell of smoke lingered but we had all settled down well and were looking forward to the second half. Alan introduced his duet with Alison and put the music on the piano for her – she'd never seen it before in her life. Glances were exchanged and after a moment's pause they sang it beautifully, Alison sight-reading the piano part and singing at the same time.

Certain topics lend themselves to a 'slide show' or at least an introduction or conclusion that uses slides. Slides are best used when you need the audience to see exactly what you are talking about: the objects, the location, the people, the circumstances. People need to see, not imagine, locations for a fund-raising event – for example, proposed sites for a residential development, pieces of furniture, slum conditions, interior design, flower collections. They are colourful, project a clean, sharp image and look professional. There are many high street reprographic specialists who will produce slides from your photographs.

Use a flip chart

Arriving early to stay overnight at the venue, I thought I would get ahead of myself and prepare my flip charts for the following day. A flip chart and stand were brought to my room as requested and I spent a productive hour or so on some colourful sheets. The steward took the stand down to the seminar room for me before breakfast. People started to arrive and I turned over to my first sheet, a 'welcome to the day' type of sheet, only to find virgin white paper; none of my stuff was there at all. A panic call to the room steward revealed that the conference steward had presumed it was old stuff from the day before and had thrown it away! The room steward searched the bins and found my prepared sheets, now with a light covering of hotel detritus, and to his eternal glory he held up the soggy sheets and read out the information for me to copy on to fresh flip chart paper.

- A flip chart is best used with a smaller audience, say up to 20 or so, otherwise a good view of it will be limited; only those nearest will be able to see it properly.

- Plan to leave plenty of white space, and leave about one-third of the page empty at the bottom. Not only is it difficult to see what's lower down the page, it's difficult to write legibly while leaning down low.

- Smooth paper and fat pens with a bullet rather than a chisel point are more comfortable and give the best result.

- Pages can be prepared ahead of time or used spontaneously.

- Dark blue and black pens work best for text and bright blue, green and red for accents and diagrams. Yellow, brown and orange don't show up well.

- You can rough out each sheet in pencil in advance; it won't show, and your writing will look spontaneous.

- Leave a blank page between each sheet so that the writing doesn't show through.

- You can put little self-stick tags on each corner to help you locate the page and to help you turn over the page more easily.

- Condense your thoughts to a few words of text; for key concepts use simple diagrams only.

- Don't underestimate the visual impact of even the most inexpertly drawn figures and diagrams.

Use an on-screen PowerPoint presentation

If you've developed the strengths of your natural style, there is no need to hide behind a PowerPoint presentation. The strengths of an on-screen presentation lie in a high level of professional impact, clever graphics (particularly flow charts and the like), colour and movement of text and images. I love PowerPoint, a marvellous bit of technology, but I've seen it abused and badly used, seen too much inappropriate material woodenly delivered, often to the wrong audience. It's interesting for the first presentation in a day, boring after the third one and we're losing the will to live after the seventh.

Use handouts and printouts of your slides

Printouts of your material are useful for you and for the audience. Your audience will have a record of your key points and any important data as well as a reminder of the visual impact. You can use them as a prompt for yourself. Print them out 1, 2, 3 or 6 to a page and then either use them to guide you through the presentation and remind you of the topics, or use them as a basis for supplementary notes if you don't feel too confident about the content. This is particularly useful when you are delivering a corporate presentation and want to personalize it.

Handouts are useful to provide details or background information. Don't give them out at the beginning; people will read them instead of paying attention to you.

Use any technology that will support, not ambush, your message

Show a video or DVD or use a camcorder, digital camera or a Polaroid camera to capture body language, facial expression or work in progress at a workshop or seminar – instant results, fun in a small to medium-sized group.

SUPPORT FOR YOUR DELIVERY

Confidence cards

◯ Key message, written out in full	Card no:
TOPIC	**Presentation aids** Slides Magazine article
Key points 1. 2. 3.	**Non-verbal cues** Pause Smile Sit down Take jacket off

Notes

	Make your notes easy to access	
1.	Get all the details down about the venue, date, time, timing, where you are in the programme and so on. Obviously it doesn't help on the day but it does help with filing and retrieval and on a really bad day helps you to focus on who you are, where you are and what you're doing there.	
2.	Set the page so that you have wide (at least 2.5cm) margins at the top, bottom and each side of the page.	
3.	**Use at least font size 16–18 (this is font size 16, bold) or as large as you need to read the print comfortably when you look at it from desk, table or lectern height, with or without your glasses.**	
4.	Use a sans-serif (without the slight projection that finishes off a stroke of a letter) font, eg **T** contrasted with T. Examples of sans-serif fonts are: **Arial**, Eras Medium, Franklin Gothic Medium, Gill Sans, Lucida Sans	
5.	Use double spacing	
6.	**Bold**	
7.	Number the points and the pages	

Use Post-it notes

A couple of Post-it notes containing key words or phrases attached to a folder or book act as unobtrusive cues. Holding on to the book or folder also helps to disguise shaky hands.

Use a photo album

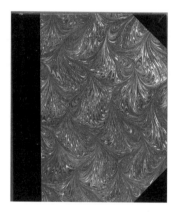

A small photo album to take 4 inch × 6 inch photos will also take index cards. If you like to walk about as you talk but are worried that you might forget what to say next, then you can hold all your prompt cards together as you walk about. If you have to deliver the same talk several times over, you can keep the cards in the same order and keep them clean.

Replace 'hide and read' with 'stand and deliver'

Hearing someone read their presentation is the most boring activity on this green earth. Never read your script unless you have to. Reading a

speech is OK if it is a formal occasion and you judge it extremely important that every word and every phrase should be heard as it was
written. Reading is OK if you have a well-modulated, expressive voice
and clear diction, don't read faster than you can speak, and have
rehearsed your script so that it sounds natural.

However, if you must read your notes verbatim:

- Go large. Print your script (or write it out legibly) so that it's large
  enough to see easily when it's placed on a table at waist height or a
  lectern at chest height. Don't hold sheets of paper if you are
  nervous. If your hands are shaking, the paper will shake as well and
  draw attention to, rather than conceal, your nerves. If there isn't a
  table available, then you could hold your notes on top of something
  substantial like a book or folder.

- Memorize your opening and closing remarks so that you don't have
  to look down.

- Look up frequently.

- Practise getting some light and shade into your voice to compensate
  for the reading.

- Don't staple the sheets together. A paper clip or folder is fine as long
  as you remove it before you start to speak.

- Slide the sheet you've just read to one side (which side depends
  whether you are right- or left-handed). Slide subsequent sheets on
  top of the first one rather than turn each page over; it looks
  smoother and more professional this way, particularly if you main-
  tain eye contact with your audience and avoid looking down at the
  sheets as you slide them across. You could also dog-ear the top or
  bottom corner of each page to help you locate and move it easily
  without fumbling. Avoid a sentence break where you turn the page.

	A. G SHEARING STAFF CONFERENCE HIGHTONE HOTEL UK 23RD NOVEMBER 2003, 08.30–16.30 **Marketing Report, third quarter 2003** 11.30–12.10pm (Following Finance Report, session chaired by Rubin Fellows)
1st slide	**Good morning everyone.** **For those of you who don't know me, let me introduce myself: 'I'm Mary Bignold and I'm an SCLM (a Senior Client Liaison Manager) in the Marketing Department at A G Shearing. I'm standing in this morning for June Treadwell, our Marketing Manager, who is unable to be with us today.** **We've been working on this quarterly report together for the last few days, so I am confident I can share the key information with you.** **Well, it's good news and bad news this quarter!** Page 1 of 7

Ring binder

Another idea is to have your notes printed out in single sheets, punch some holes and put them in a ring binder then open up the ring binder on a flat surface or lectern and just turn each page over as you come to it. Avoid a sentence break where you turn the page.

One of life's mysteries is how people who are naturally funny and engaging in an informal situation can become so awful when on a platform. I was at a conference as a delegate and met one of the speakers at dinner and was looking forward to hearing her speak the following day. The first thing that went was the voice – all individuality removed, bland, attempting to smother her regional accent. The body language was odd too, like a headteacher addressing school assembly. But worst of all, she read her script. It was an elaborate construction, dense, with textbook vocabulary and formality bordering on the regal. We then had a PowerPoint presentation in the dark. What happened to the warm, clever, amusing person we'd had supper with the night before?

6 Your setting

The setting for a beautiful diamond is designed to make the diamond appear even more beautiful. Your setting for your presentation should do the same.

When I was working as a tutor in community education I had to teach in some pretty grim environments. I never knew what would be there to greet me when I arrived. I didn't know whether the tenants' room would be clean or dirty; whether the church hall would have the heating on or not; whether the pre-school play group would have blocked the lavatories. I learnt to bring my environment with me so that the immediate area I was working in was an extension of me, my style and values and demonstrated the same standards. I didn't drive, so the instant environment had to be portable and cheap. A bunch of flowers or a jug of greenery from the garden, an Indian cotton bedspread and a few books went with me everywhere and enabled an instant transformation.

Although I rarely work in those conditions today, the principle of the travelling environment remains the same. Many corporate training rooms are bleak, many conference centres are cold and functional, many meeting rooms are untidy with irrelevant or distracting material on the walls or tables, so I still like to create a personalized mini-environment where I can.

There are three essentials to enhance your setting:

**Personalize your
environment**

**Recognize your
role and status**

**Be your own
roadie**

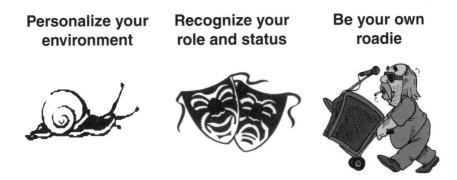

PERSONALIZE YOUR ENVIRONMENT

Like a snail or like a backpacker, you can take your house on your back; you can carry your own micro-environment with you. The first step to personalizing your environment is to accept responsibility for creating the right atmosphere. This action is about respect – respect for yourself as a professional and respect for your audience. Unless you check it out, you may not realize that the environment doesn't support your message; it may even be working against it, so do all you can do to get the environment in harmony with your style and your message.

● You can use the room, or at least part of the room, to set the tone of the occasion. Flowers, bunting, a display of literature, a box of books, a single book on a book-rest, a poster, something interesting on the flip chart, samples laid out enticingly on the table, music playing, a soft or intriguing fragrance all add to the atmosphere.

● Remove visual distractions: out of date notices, the previous occupant's notes on the flip chart or whiteboard, dirty cups, water bottles, glasses, sweet wrappings.

● Use festivals, or special days, as inspiration. Be as full on as you can get away with, depending on your style and the occasion:

  – saint's days;

  – Christmas;

  – Easter;

  – birthdays;

  – anniversaries;

  – Life–Work Balance Week;

  – Take Your Daughter to Work Day;

  – Cycle to Work Day;

  – Red Nose Day for Comic Relief.

● Best not to choose anything politically sensitive or anything that might cause offence.

My ideas occasionally backfire. I took a bunch of flowers into the training room at a site that was very cold, sleek and hi-tech. The audience was male-dominated and highly suspicious of my style and my props. I discovered later that members of the audience thought the flowers were a trick of some kind. During the coffee break they had started to take bets on what I was up to with the flowers. They couldn't concentrate on the presentation, and my simple gesture to warm up a cool environment was misunderstood and my presentation will probably be remembered for all the wrong reasons.

RECOGNIZE YOUR ROLE AND STATUS

Your role and status, along with purely practical considerations, will influence the degree to which you can manage your environment. Every situation where you have been asked to do a presentation brings its own set of circumstances. You can only manage what's yours to manage.

Role

- What part are you playing today?
- Are you the in-house speaker?
- Are you the visiting speaker brought in from outside?
- Are you speaking in your regular slot at a management meeting?
- Who will introduce you? Are you prepared to introduce yourself or reintroduce yourself if it wasn't done properly?

Status

- Are you visiting a different part of your organization or a different department?
- Are you one of many speakers or will it be just you?
- How much input do you have to the organization of the event?
- Are you the star performer, the keynote speaker? A workhorse, wheeled in to do the job you always do? A last-minute stand-in?
- Are you the light entertainment, the motivational guru, the technical expert, the fall-guy, the token male/female, there to represent the management/workers?
- Are you presenting as part of a team? Where do you fit in?

BE YOUR OWN ROADIE

I always suggest to nervous presenters that they pray for something to go wrong. Why that piece of odd advice? Because if something goes wrong and you deal with it, then it goes into your store cupboard, gets added to your stock of successes and stands you in good stead for next time, because it builds confidence based on experience. In extreme circumstances I recommend a prayer to St Jude Thaddeus – Saint of the Impossible, who takes special delight in coming to the aid of persons in desperate need. No petition seems too great for him, whence he is known as the 'Patron in Cases Despaired of'. What impresses the audience is how you deal with the situation, the way you put it right, recover and move on.

I was on second after a short break at a conference for 250 women in the City of London. I planned to start with a musical quiz, and because of technical problems at base we had recorded the excerpts on to an audio cassette instead of a CD. No problem when we did our try-out, but when I got up to speak, two things happened. First of all, the technician misread the cue to start the music and started while I was only two sentences into my introduction. Second, the volume control on the cassette player had stuck on the lowest volume; 250 people couldn't hear me or the music. After weeping silently inside at the abuse to my carefully prepared introduction, I cut it and asked for complete silence and we listened to the music, making guesses about what we could hear. When the tape was turned off and my mike back on again, I asked the audience to tell me what they thought they heard and how it related to the quiz questions. It was fun and rather silly and didn't matter a bit, and we swiftly moved on to the programme proper.

The size of the event, the importance of your contribution to the event and practical limitations such as time available, accessibility of the venue and technical requirements will determine how much work is needed from a roadie. There are some basic checks you should try to do even if you are very confident and pride yourself on dealing with the unexpected. Your secretary, your assistant, a trusted colleague or partner can all act as roadie for you. Traditionally, a roadie's role for a touring band is to check and set up equipment at the venue, but he or she will also take on whatever duties will make the performance glitch free and the performer stress free. Someone's got to do the job. See the 'Be your own roadie checklist' in Chapter 14.

Venue

- Are you going to be making the presentation in your own office, in someone else's office, in a seminar room down the corridor, in the same building, the same town, the same country, in a hotel, a conference hall?

- Are you familiar with the venue, the room, the arrangements or will you be arriving 'cold'?

- Is the venue somewhere that's used to hosting presentations or is it a bit of an ad hoc arrangement?

- What about security? Will you need a pass, a minder, a code for the door entry keypad?

- What about travel arrangements? Taxi, tickets, passport, visa?

- Do you have the full address of the venue, your room number, the telephone number, contact details of the organizer?

Script

- Have you got your script with you or do you know where to locate it quickly?

- Have you re-read your notes and got them down to a manageable set of prompts, index cards, OHPs, one page of A4 in large type or whatever works best for you?

- Are you comfortable that you can open and close your spot without looking at your notes?

Props and stage management

- Before you leave – are the props you need to illustrate your presentation in your bag or briefcase?

- If someone else is responsible for props, have you checked with him or her that the props are available?

- At the venue, are your props in the right place?

- Do you need a drink of water with you?

Sound

- Can everyone hear you? Check the sound level in the room. If others are speaking before you, listen to the quality of the sound they produce and make a note to do what they have done or else make adjustments to improve the sound.

- Is there a fixed mike, roving mike or a hand-held mike? Do you know how to use them? Do you know who to ask for help if you don't?

- Is there any background noise you will have to take into account or try to minimize?

This happened at the GMex Conference Centre in Manchester. There were 500 women for a certain roadshow and the chairperson was looking desperate. The first speaker had not turned up so would I go on? I said yes, only to discover that there was no PA system. I foolishly went on anyway and shouted for 15 minutes. The second speaker, who was cannier and more experienced than I, had time to assess the situation and learn from my mistake. She got the people sitting in the front two rows to pick up their chairs and move to the back, giving more space at the front and moving them out of an acoustically dead area defined by a heavy beam in the ceiling just above the speaker's head. She had been trained as an actor and was able to project her voice. What she did was to speak very little, but she had cleverly designed a few exercises so that the audience talked to each other, not she to them. The missing speaker and the sound system turned up at the same time.

Lighting

- Can everyone see you?
- If people are speaking before you, have you noticed or marked a spot on the floor where you can stand so that everyone can see you?
- Are there any seats with restricted views? You may want to note them and occasionally move position to give everyone a chance to see you.
- If the lighting in the room is not good, can you get more visibility by standing directly underneath whatever overhead lighting there is?

- Switch off lighting in the audience so that you can be better seen.
- Stand in front of a white screen or flip chart to create more impact if the lighting level is low.
- Don't stand in front of a window, especially if there is bright sunlight. because all the audience will see is a dark silhouette. Your face will be in shadow and you can't communicate effectively if the audience can't see your facial expression, particularly your eyes.

Costume

- Are all the clothes you intend to wear ready to go, to hand, clean, pressed?
- Have you got spares in case of emergencies?
- Is your outfit appropriate for the tone and nature of the occasion?
- Does your outfit support your key message?
- Does your outfit reflect your role for the session?

Even with my background I sometimes make the wrong costume decision. I was giving a short presentation to a group of IT consultants in a smart hotel in Oxfordshire. They were all in business dress; me, I thought as they were in IT it would be dress down day every day. I didn't look a mess but I felt embarrassed and was reminded that it's not respectful to make assumptions.

Equipment, furniture and amenities

- Does the equipment work?

- Is it arranged to best advantage?

- Locate the power supply, the on/off switch, remote switches, focus or volume knobs.

- Temperature? Best within the range of 18–22°C. The lower end will stimulate and the higher end will calm down. Above 24°C is uncomfortably warm and people might drop off to sleep or get fidgety.

- Air conditioning is a boon on sultry days but can also be very noisy or very cold. It's useful to know who knows how to control it.

- Move unwanted furniture out of audience eye-line.

- Will there be a refreshment break during your presentation? At what time? Could you arrange for it to be kept outside until you've finished speaking?

- Snacks, drinks, sweets, fruit and the like encourage informality and give an opportunity for people to chat to each other.

- Pens and paper are useful in case anyone has come under-prepared.

At a very chic conference venue in the country I arrived after the coffee break to find a slight air of panic. The earlier speaker hadn't needed any equipment and the seminar organizer was arranging the OHP ready for my slot. There was no extension lead and no power points. It was only when an emergency call to the technician was made that we discovered that all the electrical bits and pieces were under the table and that the power points were installed in the floor, also under the table – all elegantly concealed by the tablecloth.

Rehearsal

- Have you walked through how you are going to get in and out, on and off? Have you noticed what you might bump into, tread on or trip over?
- Walk through the route in your head if you can't do it for real.
- Rehearse locating, using and handling your props.
- Get the feel of the size, shape and atmosphere of the room.
- Check your 'costume' for fit and comfort if it's the first time you've worn it.

Warm-up

- Are you physically prepared? Have you got your 'relaxed but alert' routine ready?
- Use your breathing exercises to centre and focus yourself.
- Move, laugh, cough discreetly if you have been sitting silent for a while.
- Check out your PMA (positive mental attitude). Have you got your personal mantra ready? 'I am well prepared, I know what I'm talking about and I have every right to expect that things will go well.'

Get the feel of the audience

Metaphorically peep out through the curtains before a show to get a sense of the mood and atmosphere. In real terms this means taking a few moments to get the feel of the audience: are they edgy, bored, tired, up for anything, just want facts and figures, slumped, asleep, all over the place? If you're not good at picking up atmospheres, leave this bit out, you won't know what's going on anyway; focus on projecting yourself and looking for a few bright faces to alight on.

Emergencies, repair kit, supplies

Some people like to take a full emergency kit. I prefer to contact the venue in advance and just take my personal favourites.

- A pack of non-smear glass wipes is useful. Many projectors have dirty screens or lenses, which makes your stuff look unprofessional although it's not your fault.

- A cross-head screwdriver.

- Wide Sellotape – useful for taping down stray wires and for getting rid of dust and fluff.

- Favourite felt tip pens – corporate or conference-supplied felt tip pens can be horrible: scratchy or dried up or with too skinny a point. A basic pack of four (two black, one blue, one red) won't take up much room.

At the very least, double-check the day before a big presentation that everything is still on course and that you have your materials ready packed, the date, time and venue details correct plus a contact number in case of emergencies.

7   Your delivery

It's an exhilarating feeling when you are completely relaxed and confident while giving a presentation. When you feel you can go anywhere you like and the audience will come with you. When you can dance with the options in your head and know you will choose the right one. When your gestures are natural and forceful, when your face is alight and you project energy and charisma. When you are being yourself – not performing, not making a speech, not 'presenting'. You then realize why brilliant public speakers can command huge fees. They can't have an off day. They have to be like that all the time.

Imagine a game of snakes and ladders, like the one pictured, which is from the Bangladesh Museum in Canada. A throw of the dice, a successful presentation and you travel up a ladder. Lack of opportunities to practise, a negative presentation experience, an unexpected professional setback, perceived failure or criticism or loss of personal direction could mean you slide down the snake. This can result in temporary loss of confidence, loss of self-esteem and an unwillingness to take risks. Then another opportunity arises and with it a chance to go up the ladder again.

> **'A good presentation is a mixture of total relaxation and total concentration.'**
>
> *(Anon)*

THE FOUR STAGES OF SPEAKING

Like an alcoholic, a presenter is either suffering or in recovery. Your delivery will rely very much on what stage of public speaking you have reached. Bert Decker, in *High Impact Communication*, published by Nightingale Conant Corporation, USA, describes all communicators as being sited in one of the four stages of speaking. Advancing from one stage to the next requires an effort of will, taking a few risks, as well as getting some presentation skills training.

1. The non-speaker

People at this stage avoid public speaking at all costs. They experience a feeling of terror at the thought and find excuses not to do it. Typically, they get anxious if the job requires speaking skills.

2. The occasional speaker

People at this level accept with reluctance any invitations to speak. They recognize that they must be able to present their ideas if they are to get on in their career, so they will speak if they have to. They still feel fear, but the fear is inhibiting, not disabling. This is the easiest stage to advance from just by getting more practice in speaking in public.

3. The willing speaker

Fear is not a drawback at this level, but the willing speaker experiences tension that he or she finds annoying, not inhibiting. At this level people are willing to speak their minds in meetings and are prepared to put themselves to the fore. They speak often and can be articulate and confident in front of an audience.

4. The communicator

Communicators find speaking to an audience stimulating. They are driven to present themselves and their ideas. They speak up and speak out in all situations. They have the ability to inspire and motivate. They have learnt to turn adrenaline into positive energy.

If speaking in public is your worst fear and exposure to it, even if successful, doesn't reduce the fear, then I believe you shouldn't torment yourself. Find a job that doesn't require these skills. Be kind to yourself.

Or... take a risk. Throw the dice. Push on to the next level. It might be a ladder.

'Men acquire a particular quality by constantly acting a particular way... you become just by performing just actions,
temperate by performing temperate actions, brave by
performing brave actions.'

(Aristotle, 384–322 BC)

PRESENCE AND IMPACT

If your body is there but it has lost contact with your brain because you
are nervous, apprehensive or indulging in negative self-talk, you won't
be able to deliver your material. You can't make an impact; you can't
have 'presence' if you're not 'there'.

GETTING RID OF THE GREMLINS

Delivering the presentation is the whole point of the preparation: the
sleepless nights, all that reading and rehearsing. Doing it is what it's all
about. The good news is that if you've done all that preparation, planning and rehearsal you should be fine. However, it's often at this stage
that your gremlins pay you a visit.

Your gremlin is the voice in your head that specializes in negative self-
talk. Your gremlin wants you to fail, saps your confidence by telling you

how silly or stupid or sad you are and may encourage you to relive previous failures, to forget joys, to avoid risk and serves to make you feel inadequate, incompetent, ugly or uncomfortable. If your gremlin decides to visit you while you are planning your presentation or even while you are performing, you need a gremlin zapping technique.

COME TO YOUR SENSES

Concentrating on the information your senses are bringing to you in the here and now will stop negative anticipation and keep the gremlins at bay. This will keep your heart rate activity low and keep you securely in the moment so that when the time comes to speak, you are 'present'. The following exercise can be done minutes before you start your presentation, or even earlier – on the train, for example, in a corridor or in the cloakroom. You just do as much of it as you can, in the time that you have, to suit the circumstances.

1. Sit with your back straight, knees slightly apart, feet flat on the floor, hands resting lightly on your knees.

2. Breathe slowly in and out, in through your nose and out through your mouth.

3. Imagine breathing in a clear, blue, clean light and breathing out a grey, brown dust, clearing out the rubbish and negative talk.

4. Be aware of your skin enveloping your muscles and internal organs, head to foot.

5. Focus your senses one by one. If you have had your eyes closed while you were breathing, open them now and start to talk to yourself in your head.

6. What you can see? Don't analyse, criticize or interpret; just describe what you can see directly in front of you. A row of heads,

short blonde hair, a bald head, a blue shirt collar, long silver earrings, a tattoo?

7. What can you hear? Another speaker's voice, the clatter of glasses from the bar, the breathing of the person next to you, your heart beating, the scratch of a pen on paper, the hum of the air conditioning, laughter from outside?

8. What can you feel? The leather of the chair you're sitting on, the texture of your trousers on your legs, the inside of your shoes, your shirt collar at your neck, the smooth finish of the plastic folder on your lap, your tongue in your mouth, a sharp edge to a tooth?

9. What can you taste? Your toothpaste, the coffee you had at the station, your lipstick?

10. What can you smell? A faint trace of your own perfume, a stale burger, rain, newsprint, the carpet, paint, cleaning product, air freshener?

11. Return to the external world when you're ready – gremlins zapped!

WARM-UP

A warm-up before a performance is absolutely vital. Actors do it. Athletes do it. Musicians do it. As businesspeople, do we do it? Of course we should; it is crass and arrogant not to. How you choose to warm up depends on the circumstances, mainly to do with how visible you are and how nervous you've become. Some warm-ups are best executed in private, or at least quietly and invisibly. If you can find a few minutes' privacy you can let rip!

● See Chapter 8 for ideas on how to do a psychological warm-up.

- See Chapter 9 for ideas on how to do a vocal warm-up.
- See Chapter 10 for ideas on how to do a physical warm-up.

MAKING AN ENTRANCE

Knowing how to get on and get off again is a great survival tool in the presentation game. Whether you are just presenting a few ideas at a team meeting or making a specialist input to a big conference, your impact depends on how you open and close your spot. If you have to walk to your position and you have not been able to put your stuff in place before you start, hold your notes, slides, props, books and so on in one hand or tucked under the same arm to look more collected. When you hear your name and you know you are on next, the important thing to remember is to pause. In that pause you give yourself a few seconds to focus:

- Breathe in slowly and breathe out slowly – remember to b-l-o-w the out breath.
- Bite the tip of your tongue to get the saliva flowing.
- Check you have your notes in front of you, place your finger or a pen where you will start.
- Look up.
- Make eye contact round the room.
- Look for the 'bright faces'.
- Smile.
- Start.
- Begin positively on an upbeat note.

- Rehearse your opening remarks so that you don't have to look down at your notes.

WHPSIE

Walk like a winner, head up, chin up, shoulders down, easy pace. Hands under control. Make eye contact. Pause – remember the power of the pause. Smile. Inhale, exhale. Engage brain.

MAKING AN EXIT

Your closing remarks and exit will have more impact if they are delivered with composure. Making eye contact with the audience and smiling before you go leaves them with a positive impression. When you have come to the end of your presentation and spoken the final sentence, resist the temptation to rush off. If you have rehearsed your closing remarks, you won't need to look at your notes for this part. Even if you are relieved to have got it over with, letting it show doesn't look very professional. Pause, acknowledge the applause with a smile or a nod or a bow if it's that kind of occasion; otherwise, keep your head up, make eye contact, smile and either sit down or ask for questions or wait for the chair to ask for questions. Collect your bits and pieces, transfer them to one hand or put them under one arm and start to move off *after* you have said your last word. Don't rush. Walk away smartly or sit down with a minimum of fuss. *Don't speak and walk at the same time; it reduces your impact to zero.*

CLOSING YOUR PRESENTATION

Advice to potential speakers from an experienced chair:

> **'Never close your presentation at one of our meetings with the words: "... and finally ladies..."** Your closing words will be drowned by the sound of several hundred handbags snapping shut.'**

(Past Regional Chair, The Women's Institute)

The PLUS exit strategy

Pause, Look Up, Smile

Then, gather your notes and get off!

VISUAL IMPACT

Your appearance

You have the most marvellous opportunity to enhance your presentation in obvious and subtle ways through the way you look. The audience will only criticize how you look if they get bored. Check your appearance before you go on. Use a full-length mirror if possible. Pay special attention to your grooming.

- Decide how informal or casual you would like to appear. Choose an outfit that is congruent with your message – it isn't always appropriate to be booted and suited. Who in the audience do you most want to influence? Choose your outfit to impress them.

- Formality in dress means sober colours, with a well-defined shoulder-line kept clear of hair, scarves and fussy details. Wear a tailored jacket; keep it buttoned up. Wear a suit and tie.

- Avoid visual distractions to your main verbal message; don't choose anything too short, too tight or too see-through.

- Wear clothes that are comfortable, that you can move about in and will absorb sweat if you are an active presenter. A big presentation is not the right time to try out a new look or a new outfit unless your confidence is high.

- If your presentation ideas are radical ones, consider *either* making them appear even more radical by wearing a radical outfit *or* toning down the message with a conservative outfit, so that you don't fire too many shots at once.

- Check the background. Will you merge into it or stand out? A beige jacket will look great in front of corporate blue panels, but insignificant against light wood panelling.

- Over-bright clothes, fashion forward items and strong styling will overpower the message.

- A small audience requires a non-threatening presence, especially if you are all sitting close together.

At a public meeting about environmental issues, including refuse collection, street cleansing and recycling, on comes Brian wearing a beautifully ironed Saturday morning casual shirt (in contrast to the councillors, who were wearing tired weekday suits). He was a big, comfortable, confident, competent-looking chap, and you knew you were in safe hands.

See Chapter 14 for a Top-to-Toe Visual Impact Checklist.

If you have a minute to spare:

- Run your hands and wrists hands under cold water to cool down.

- Have a quick spray of breath freshener.

- Have a spray of your favourite scent (if it's not overpowering) to boost your confidence.

Your body language

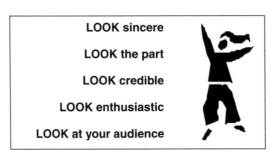

LOOK sincere

LOOK the part

LOOK credible

LOOK enthusiastic

LOOK at your audience

Your whole body should look as though it is involved with the performance, not just your mouth opening and shutting:

- **Natural gestures.** Using spontaneous, natural hand gestures adds life and emphasis to a presentation. As a general rule, keep your hand movements below shoulder level unless you are in front of a big audience or you have a big point to make.

- **Eye contact.** Make eye contact with one or two people immediately and everyone in the audience at some time during the presentation.

- **Facial expression.** A friendly facial expression is an open one. Openness is attractive and looks confident. Lift your forehead and eyebrows to remove a possible frown. If your teeth are clenched, unclench them.

- **Smile.** A genuine smile lights up you face. A nervous smile puts you in victim mode. One or two genuine smiles will work better than a nervous smile every few minutes.

- **Look relaxed and informal.** Sit on a stool; lean lightly on the back of a chair.

- **Move towards, not away from, your audience.** Walking or moving backwards looks as though you are intimidated by or unsure of your audience.

- **Be relaxed and ready.** 'Plant' yourself in front of the audience to begin with: feet about 30~cm apart, pointing straight ahead or in third position in ballet, hands loosely at your sides, shoulders down, chin up, don't look at your feet. This is the 'ready' position from which you can move naturally in any direction.

- **Have a 'home base'.** If you tend to wander about when you talk (and there's nothing intrinsically wrong with that), you might occasionally want to give yourself and your audience a rest. Choose a spot that you return to now and again, where you stay still, assuming the ready position for a few seconds or a few minutes before moving off again.

FEEDBACK

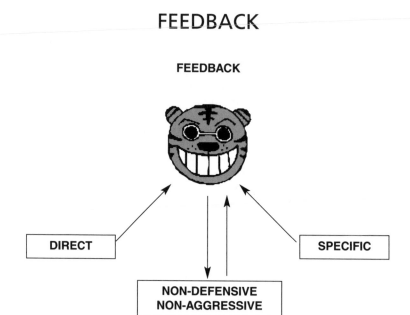

Did you achieve your objective? Well, how will you know? Ask yourself: How will I know what my audience has done, if anything, as a result of my presentation? Check audience response against your objectives for the presentation. There are various methods for getting the answers: ask colleagues, audience members, do a survey, a straw poll, a questionnaire. Set something up in advance or just trust to luck after the event.

If you have spent time, effort and emotional energy on a presentation, you may want to get some feedback about how you did. You could look at it on video or listen to it on tape and evaluate your delivery for yourself. Alternatively, you could ask the opinion of someone who was in the audience. Looking at yourself through the eyes of others can provide critical insight into how your behaviour has been interpreted.

In its simplest, but very useful, form, feedback from someone else tells you how you came across to that person – not everyone in the audience, just him or her. Yet feedback can be threatening. The dilemma we face is that we're curious about how other people view us, but the thought of actually finding out can make us nervous and apprehensive. Start assertively by positioning your request for feedback to make it as easy as possible for the person to give you what you want.

Ask the person who is going to give you feedback to award you marks out of 10 for 1) **technical merit** – could they see, hear, understand? How did the presentation rate for logical order, clarity of purpose, clarity of delivery, etc; and then for 2) **artistic impression** – entertainment value, how interesting the content was, use of support material, what you were wearing, etc.

- Choose someone you trust – a workmate, team member, senior colleague, boss or mentor – and invite him or her to support you. Most people would be delighted to help. If you have a coach or buddy, then this is an ideal job for such a person if it's appropriate for her to attend the presentation.

- Put your request into context. Maybe you'd like some feedback because improving your presentation skills is part of your personal development plan or you'd like colleagues or clients to see you in a different role.

- Tell your colleague why you have chosen him or her and what you would like him or her to do.

  Be specific about what you want him or her to comment on. For example:

  - 'I've been working really hard on maintaining eye contact throughout the early stages of my presentation. Will you tell me what you saw me do?'

  - 'I would like to appear more relaxed and have been experimenting with some breathing techniques and trying a different way of standing that I think does this. Will you tell me what you notice?'

- 'I have a tendency to go off at a tangent. Can you tell me whether I stuck to my plan or wandered off?'

● If you want to gain a more general impression about how you came across, then ask for three things the feedback giver liked about your presentation and two things you could have done differently to make it more appealing. The key questions are:

- What did you see?

- What did you hear?

- What did you sense?

● What isn't helpful is either a sycophantic response or a heap of negative criticism. Saying, 'You were wonderful' to avoid hurting your feelings is just as bad as a 10-page report detailing your presentational inadequacies.

● Resist the temptation to defend what you did or what you said. Say 'thank you', store the comments away and learn from them if you can.

At its best, feedback is:

● not given or received defensively;

● not given or received aggressively;

● direct: face-to-face, not second-hand or via a third party;

● specific: about the observation of previously agreed behaviours.

The easiest way to adopt a non-aggressive or non-defensive attitude as a feedback giver is to choose your feedback language carefully. For example: *'I noticed that you said...'* or *'This made me feel that...'* or *'This made me think that…' or 'One thing I might have done differently with that audience is…'*

The easiest way to adopt non-defensive or non-aggressive behaviour as a receiver is just to smile, say thank you and then shut up!

Measure the **snooze factor** of your presentation by positioning yourself on the Snooze-Meter. See Chapter 14, Checklists and Formats.

8 Your confidence

'There's nothing wrong with you that what's right with you can't fix.'

(Anon)

It's natural to feel fear or anxiety when on unfamiliar territory. Fear of making a presentation comes from your ego. Conquering the fear of speaking in public comes from preparation, rehearsal and experience: just doing it and getting better at it; noticing what went well, what went badly, how you felt about it, what feedback you got, how you dealt with things that went wrong. Being audience-centred rather than self-centred turns your focus outward instead of inward. Your focus moves away from doubts and fears and towards the enjoyment of sharing knowledge and making connections with people – setting up creative apprehension, not fear. The best confidence trick in the world is to appear relaxed, authoritative, controlled and assured when you are deeply nervous. Reframe your fears. As prevention is often better than cure, here is a list of ideas that might help.

WHAT GIVES YOU CONFIDENCE?

The following are all factors that will give you confidence:

- having self-belief – the confidence that you have something of value to offer;
- looking good;
- being well prepared;
- having approval;
- being relaxed;
- knowing what you're talking about;
- knowing what's going to happen;
- being familiar with the environment;
- having plenty of time;
- having a challenge;
- competition.

WHAT MAKES YOUR CONFIDENCE RUN LOW?

The following are factors that can sap your confidence:

- lack of preparation;
- not knowing the audience;
- lack of sleep;
- not having the right clothes;
- having a bad hair day;

- being undermined;
- working to someone else's script;
- being unfamiliar with the environment;
- being wrong, or wrong-footed;
- having to be someone you're not.

CONFIDENCE CURRENCIES

Make sure you have the right confidence currencies available so that you can 'buy' whatever you need that makes you feel confident:

- **People.** Make it up if you've had a row before you go to work.
- **Money.** If looking good matters to you, book in a haircut or a mani-cure; pay the baby-sitter an extra hour.
- **Time.** Preparation and rehearsal are legitimate business activities, so make time in your diary for thinking and planning.
- **Effort.** Get up an hour earlier to make sure all is OK at the venue.

DO YOU WANT TO IMPROVE YOUR PERFORMANCE?

- Focus on one skill at a time. Be like a circus plate-spinner: add one plate at a time until you can manage to spin them all at once.
- Volunteer to make a presentation as often as you can.
- Get objective and subjective feedback. Learn from it; grow. Realize your potential.

- Ask more of yourself.
- Take a few risks. Move out of your comfort zone occasionally. Put yourself, your ideas, your style on the line. High risk, high reward.
- Let your natural style free.
- Don't take it all too seriously.

TALK TO YOURSELF

Pre-presentation self-talk

Prepare your personal mantra: 'I know what I'm talking about, I'm well prepared and I have every right to expect that things will go well.'

During-the-presentation self-talk

'I'm still standing' (think Elton John), 'I'm breathing, I'm speaking, I'm taking one step at a time.'

Post-presentation self-talk

'I'm really pleased with the way I handled that last tricky question.' 'I can learn how to manage my material better from the way the audience responded to the first section.'

> **'If you think you can, you can.**
> **If you think you can't, you're right.'**
>
> *(Mary Kay)*

HANDLING NERVES

Deborah Bull, a leading British ballet dancer, once described how she felt following a leg injury. She was having trouble getting her confidence back and was extremely nervous even though she was step-perfect and performing a familiar work. She was worried that her injury would prevent her from doing a particular step. She realized that her world of worry was reduced to this single step and she felt as though she was 'wading through glue in the dark'. The realization was enough: she went on and danced – beautifully.

WHAT MAKES YOU NERVOUS?

What could stop you giving the best presentation you can? Most people would answer by saying that their nerves would get the better of them. Nerves come from fear:

- Fear of being judged – 'The audience will think I'm awful, that I can't do my job, can't deliver a simple presentation, that I'm arrogant, that I'm feeble.'

- Fear of rejection – 'The audience won't like me.'

- Fear of failure – 'I will fail to get my message across, the audience might not understand me or resist my plans, dislike my ideas.'

- Forgetting – 'I will forget what I want to say, lose my place, make mistakes, go blank.'

- Fidgeting – 'I might use inappropriate body language and gestures, which will make me look nervous, insecure or overconfident.'

- Fluffing and flannelling – 'Instead of being clear and direct, I will either be tongue-tied or over-loquacious.'

- Feeling a fool – 'I suspect the audience won't like me, they will think I don't know what I'm talking about, they're bound to know more than me.'
- Feeling frightened of the audience – 'They might interrupt me, confuse me, be hostile to me, ask awkward questions.'

SYMPTOMS

The following are the physical symptoms of nervousness:

- dry mouth;
- shaking knees;
- trembling hands;
- not knowing what to do with your hands;
- sweating;
- feeling sick;
- loose bowels;
- squeaky voice;
- behaving in an uncharacteristic manner, eg being too loud, too meek, gushing, over-familiar, excessively formal.

These fears and their associated symptoms are very common, and most speakers experience fears like this at least to begin with, if not to some degree for ever. Such fears are not experienced by people who are either innocent or arrogant. The innocents are usually unselfconscious with a low level of self-awareness and are ignorant of possible pitfalls, blithely thinking they will be all right. Conversely, the arrogant ones' lack of self-awareness prevents them from accepting that they might need to change because they perceive themselves to be fine as they are, and they have no idea of how they might coming across.

For the rest of us, nerves are normal. Work through what makes you nervous and get some form of control over those factors. It won't ever be total control. You need a little rush of adrenaline to give you a stimulus to perform.

See Chapter 2, 'Be your own presentation skills doctor'.

DON'T BE A 'VICTIM IN WAITING' – OVERCOME YOUR NERVES

1. Lay your worst horror on the line. What is the worst thing that can happen to you during your presentation?

2. Is it a realistic fear? Why?

3. Is it an unrealistic fear? Why?

4. Work it through step by step:

    - What will the consequences be?

    - What will the audience think?

    - How will you cope?

    - What will you do to remove the cause of the fear?

    - What will you do to remove the fear?

5. Imagine your kind of success for yourself.

6. Make the kind of preparations that give you the most confidence.

7. Take control, don't be a 'victim in waiting'

PREVENTION MECHANISMS

- Deal with a mistake with the minimum of fuss. The chances are, no one has noticed. Fix it and move on. This is the way to show confidence and professionalism.

- Don't try to learn a script by heart. If you miss a line or a phrase, there's a danger that you will forget altogether where you are.

- Practise aloud any unfamiliar or unusual words or phrases. The presentation itself shouldn't be the first occasion you hear them.

- Use your notes when you practise so that you are familiar with them even if you don't use them on the day.

- If you've made notes, have them conveniently by you. They will keep you on track if you lose your place, so that you can follow them even if you aren't actively using them.

- Include details, quotations and data in their full form in your notes so that you can refer to them quickly and easily if your memory fails you.

- Most people in the audience won't notice a small or even a big mistake if you handle it smoothly.

RESCUE MECHANISMS

Forgetting what you intended to say

Buy time, make a thoughtful pause, locate your notes, take a breath in and gently release it, find your place and continue. No one will notice unless you draw it to their attention.

Forgetting a word

We all do it; even the simplest, most commonly used word escapes us from time to time. Sometimes it happens when you ad lib; you didn't intend to include that particular story or that reference in the presentation so you haven't rehearsed it. Sometimes your mind is racing ahead of your mouth and you fall over, mentally. If you have an informal style, the easiest thing to do is just to ask the audience – the advantage is an unexpected bit of audience participation as well as the word you were searching for.

Going blank

Going blank often occurs when you have lost focus, your mind has gone off somewhere and you are not fully 'present' in the situation. Go back to the point you were making before you went blank, locate your place in your notes and continue.

Losing your place

Move your body, change your position, relocate yourself physically and you will probably relocate yourself mentally. If it's taking you a few moments and it's become obvious what's happening, you can light-heartedly mention what's going on rather than try to cover it up. You can make a joke about it (preferably one you have prepared earlier). You can always skip the point you were going to make and move on. (Don't share this bit with the audience.)

Factual mistake, slip of the tongue

The audience often realize that what you said was a mistake and won't make an issue of it, knowing that you had not meant to deceive or hurt people's feelings. Use humour, smile, put your mistake right, just a knowing look can often enable you and the group to laugh it off and move on quickly.

Offending someone

If it is obvious that some people in the group are hurt or offended, then admit responsibility for the mistake and emphasize the innocence of the remark. Don't make a list of excuses; apologize and move on. If you think you might have accidentally offended one or two people in the group, admit the mistake in private as soon as an opportunity arises after the presentation.

PSYCHOLOGICAL WARM-UP

1. Take your 'seven stars' with you (see Chapter 1).

2. Visualize yourself as calm and in control, exuding energy and enthusiasm.

3. Picture yourself as knowledgeable, witty and confident.

4. 'Own' the stage. Mentally use up all the space around you and fill it.

5. Use a mental mantra: tell yourself you are well prepared, you know what you're talking about and that you are going to enjoy yourself.

PART II

Creative preferences

9 Sound

We are surrounded by sounds and music all our waking life. We get woken by musical alarm clocks, listen to the radio while we shower, hear Muzak in lifts, hear the 'no tune, no rhythm' music in health spas. Then there is traffic noise, computer hum, building works, buskers, background music in pubs, clubs, bars and restaurants, music as a commuter soundtrack at railway stations. People talk to us and we relax by listening to CDs and DVDs. Audio-sensitive people get a buzz from sound in a way that other people don't. An audio-sensitive presenter may have an interesting voice, may ask you to listen to material or play you music.

Are you an 'audio' person?	YES	NO	SOMETIMES
1. Do you enjoy listening to music, plays, talk programmes on the radio?			
2. Would you sometimes like to be read to rather than read for yourself?			
3. Do you prefer to give verbal directions and instructions?			
4. Do you talk a lot and have a wide vocabulary?			
5. Can you sing, remember tunes, sing in tune?			
6. Do you like music in the background when you are working?			
7. Do you express how you feel through your tone of voice?			
8. Do you use rhythm or rhyme to remember things such as a shopping list or telephone number?			
9. Can you recall people's names easily?			
10. Can you recall facts easily?			
TOTALS			

Here are some ways to incorporate sound creatively into your presentation style.

MUSIC AND SINGING

Research has shown that the most effective music to listen to in terms of helping you to learn academic material is the music of the Classical and Baroque period. Bach, Vivaldi and Mozart in particular have a consistent tempo and the most impact.

'A Baroque andante helps calm an overbeating heart. These composers seem to follow the natural geometry of sound, echoing the harmonic relationships in nature.'

(*Olivea Dewhurst-Maddock,* Healing with Sound, *1988*)

Dip into these ideas. Find something you haven't tried before and make it work for you.

Energize a group

Find some bright, stimulating, rhythmic music. Surprise yourself and research outside your favourites. Try disco music, steel bands, salsa, brass bands, marches, drums. Try 'Pump It Up' by Elvis Costello, 'Teddy Bear' by Elvis Presley, the 'Russian Dance' from the *Nutcracker Suite* by Tchaikovsky, the 'Grand March' from Verdi's *Aida*.

Calm down

If you want to calm your nerves before a presentation, you could put your headphones on for four or five minutes and play some relaxing music: cool jazz, lullabies, Gregorian chant, the slow movements from any of the big classical symphonies, a Chopin nocturne.

Conduct an imaginary orchestra

Get the group to stand up and conduct an imaginary orchestra to a lively piece of music as an after-lunch livener.

Play an instrument to close your presentation

A popular presenter I have come across closes his session at conference by playing his guitar.

Play a 'Name that Tune' game

Play a few bars of popular tunes for the audience to guess. Use as an introduction or a warm up.

Manage the mood

Play an excerpt of music at some point in a presentation, workshop, seminar or meeting. I've used popular songs as an upbeat start to a presentation and to mark the key points of the presentation. In a presentation about career development, the audience had to answer the question 'What do you really want?' in the form of a musical quiz:

- Success? To be the best? 'Simply the Best', Tina Turner;
- Power? 'If I Had a Hammer', Trini Lopez;
- To love and be loved? 'Love Me Tender', Elvis Presley;

- Fame, public recognition? 'Razzle Dazzle 'em', from the musical Chicago;

- Money? 'Give Me Money', the Beatles;

- Peace? 'Give Peace a Chance', John Lennon.

Set a concept to music

For example, try finding a song for each level of Maslow's hierarchy of needs:

- self-actualization: 'I Am What I Am', from the musical La Cage aux Folles; 'I Did It My Way', Frank Sinatra;

- self-esteem:

- social:

- safety:

- food and water:

Sing

Singing is a wonderful way to lift your spirits and boost your confidence. As part of your preparation plan you can sing aloud to music to really get your energy levels up and improve the quality of your speaking voice. You can sing along to anything that appeals to you: children's songs, rock anthems, operatic arias, popular choruses, love songs, folk songs, hymns.

Singing helps release endorphins – the chemicals in the brain that lift your mood. It doesn't matter if you can't sing in tune or reach all the notes, it's the energy and feeling that count. However, you'll feel better about yourself if you select songs that are not in too high or too low a key for you, songs that you know all the words to or at least can pick up quickly, and songs that don't have too many tricky bits that you keep leaving out. This is why choosing hymns and carols will work because they were written for a mass audience who weren't necessarily trained singers and had a limited vocal range.

You could try:

- 'Abide with Me', 'There Is a Green Hill Far Away', 'Lord of the Dance', 'While Shepherds Watched Their Flocks by Night'.

- Any of the big rock anthems such as 'We Are the Champions', Queen.

- Something gentle such as 'Love Me Tender' or 'Are you Lonesome Tonight?' from Elvis Presley's repertoire would be good for controlling your breathing and would help you to enunciate every word clearly.

- Something tuneful such as any Neapolitan folk songs sung by Pavarotti – even if you can't sing them in Italian, if you know the tune, pom pom and la la your way through and release some emotion and *hwyl* (heart).

- Anything from Robbie Williams's *Sing While You're Winning* album.

Other suggestions

- **Sing in the car.** On the way to make your presentation, whether it's at an interview, sales conference, board meeting or whether you're giving a lecture, running a workshop or having a team briefing, having a good loud sing can enhance your mood as well as loosen up your voice and improve your breathing.

- **Sing in the shower.** With or without the radio, sing along just for the pleasure of it.

- **Take in a karaoke machine.**

- **Develop your personal music collection** specially for presentations.

VOICE QUALITY

Your vocal tone – the quality of your voice – is the carrier of what you say. Your tone of voice reflects how you feel – your mood and current emotional state – and is a strong part of your presentation persona. Your vocal tone can make you sound sarcastic, subservient, superior, terrified, timid or tetchy.

Dip into these ideas. Find something serendipitous you haven't tried before and make it work for you.

- **Diction.** Look after the consonants and the vowels will look after themselves.

- **Funny voice.** If you are a good mimic and have an ear for how people talk, introduce a foreign accent, character voice or regional accent (if appropriate).

- **Recorded speech.** There are many resources available for finding recordings of famous speeches, interviews with celebrities, plays and readings from novels.

- **Rhythm.** Introduce rhythm to avoid flatness or monotony.

- **Silence.** Silence is as powerful as sound if it's carefully used as a contrast.

- **Pace.** Make a note in your script to change gear occasionally and increase or decrease the speed at which you're speaking.

- **The power of the pause.** Pause before a word for emphasis, before starting on a new topic, before you start and before you close down.

- **Pitch.** Nerves make the pitch of your voice rise. Bring it down a little by speaking on the out breath, not the in breath.

- **Listen to recordings of well-known speakers.** There's a lot to be learnt from poets, storytellers and others for whom the spoken word is their livelihood. Listen to the phrasing, the tone and the rhythm.

- **Vocalizations.** The sounds and noises we make that are not language, eg ums and errs, hums and ha's, sighing, tutting, whistling, coughing and throat clearing, can subtract from your vocal impact. Check how many of these non-words you habitually use. If over-used, they can become irritating.

  - Eliminate RPs (repetitive phrases): 'Like...', 'Y'know...', 'Know what I mean?'

  - Eliminate VSs (verbal softeners): 'I don't know why I've been asked to talk to you about this...', 'I'm only the...', 'I'm really not too sure...', 'I'll have to check with...', 'I could be mistaken but...'

- Eliminate VFs (vocal fillers): 'um', 'err', 'dit de dit', 'ch, ch, ch'.

● **Volume.** Why don't you turn the volume of your voice up unexpectedly to emphasize a key word, or turn the volume down to a whisper so that your audience has to strain to hear it? This is the power of aural contrast at work. It will emphasize that word or phrase and, as a bonus, bring back the attention of anyone who has mentally wandered off.

● **Water.** A glass of water at room temperature laced with a little honey is kinder to your voice than iced water or fizzy water, which will only make you burp.

● **Sound effects.** It's useful to have some sound effects to create mood or to mark the different sections of your presentation:

- percussive (body): clap hands, pat thighs, stamp feet;

- percussive (instrument): drum, bells, triangle, tambourine, maracas, rattle, bubble wrap.

● **Get into a band.** Ask your audience to form an impromptu band using only percussive instruments. Find out if anyone can conduct and start with a simple rhythm and build it up, with improvisation. This raises energy levels, is good for team-building and cooperative effort... and is very funny.

● **Time's up.** Find a CD with sound effects to help you indicate the time allowed for thinking or discussion; for example:

- clock ticking, alarm;

- countdown for 30 seconds, one minute, five minutes;

- referee's whistle;

- police or ambulance siren.

- **Set the mood.** You can use:
    - whale song;
    - the sea breaking over pebbles;
    - birdsong (the National Trust has several CDs of birdsong);
    - weather: rain, wind, thunder.
- **Vocal warm-up:**
    - Waggle your jaw from side to side to loosen it up so that your speech is clear.
    - Chew an imaginary apple for the same effect.
    - Blow raspberries to loosen your lips.
    - Get someone to make you laugh. Laughing reduces tension and relaxes key muscles in the stomach, shoulders and face so you have a more natural stance and expression.
    - Sing up and down a few scales, exercising your lips and tongue: la-la-la-la-la-la-la-la, me-me-me-me-me-me-me-me-me, too-too-too-too-too-too-too-too-too.
    - Make an aside to someone before you start to speak, so that if you need to cough or clear your throat you have the opportunity then, not when you begin your presentation.

10 Movement

Physical movement is very important to kinetic presenters. You will see them pacing the platform as they speak, or walking about the room at a meeting as they sort through a problem in their heads. If they are forced to stand in one place or sit still, it can have an adverse effect on their presentation style. They are often uncomfortable in formal clothes and can seen sweating, pulling and tugging at their clothes or struggling with shirts coming out of their trousers, shirt button undone at the neck and loose tie. Using movement and physicality in a presentation is a freedom for those who prefer a kinetic style, and can be energizing for the audience.

Are you a 'kinetic' person? How 'physical' are you?	YES	NO	SOMETIMES
1. Do you take part in sports activities or some kind of physical exercise? Do you need to move your body frequently?			
2. Do you quite like a bit of horse-play with your kids?			
3. Would you say you were quite good at DIY?			
4. Can you mend and make things?			
5. Do you like to use your brain to think about dilemmas or problems while doing something physical such as running, swimming, ironing or walking?			
6. Do you get up and dance at a club or at a party?			
7. Do you enjoy going for walks, having a swim?			
8. Do you like to physically get hold of something in order to understand how to use it or do it?			
9. Do you choose furniture, clothes on their comfort or "feel" factor?			
10. Do you like to show someone how to do something rather than tell them or draw a diagram for them?			
TOTALS			

Dip into these ideas. Find something you haven't tried before and make it work for you.

● **Be larger than life.** Use all 'your' space. Think and feel a balloon all round you. Reach up and touch the edge of the space with your fingers, in front, to the side and to the back. It's all yours.

● **Move to emphasize differences, sequences.** On the one hand – you move to one side; on the other hand – you move to the other. If you were explaining something to an audience that was in four discrete sections, you could jump or move to each quadrant of a set of imaginary squares like carpet tiles. Or move sideways.

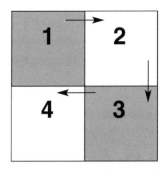

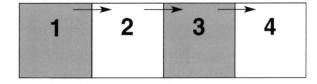

● **Move, change position.** Give yourself time to think.

● **Move from one side of the stage, room or platform area to another.** This gives people with different visual and hearing dominances a chance to receive you on their wavelength.

- **The 'one hand trick'.** If you don't know what to do with your hands, because either you are a fidgeter or you tend to be bit wooden with your hands hanging down, stuck to your sides, then try the 'one hand trick'. This involves finding a suitable place to put one hand while you gesture comfortably with the other. You could place one hand in your pocket (no coins, no keys), on the side of the lectern, on the table or on the back of a chair.

- **Mannerisms.** Watch out for any mannerisms you may have developed.

- **Posture and stance** can influence audience perception.

How to appear informal	How to appear formal
Sitting on edge of table	Standing upright
Moving away from lectern or table	Remaining at lectern
Walking about	Standing still
Leaning against lectern	Body away from the lectern
Hands in pockets	Hands resting on sides of lectern
Plenty of hand gestures	Few gestures
Taking off jacket, loosening tie	Jacket buttoned up
Useful for	**Useful for**
Workshops	Junior to senior
Facilitating, not lecturing	Conveying authority
Senior to junior	Conveying strength
Establishing a friendly atmosphere	Serious situation
Appearing relaxed	Hostile audience

- **The Hollywood pause.** Have you noticed how the 'stars' in a film get an opportunity to face the camera for a last shot before the scene changes? The shot will show their best facial angle and their figure to advantage. This usually involves a door frame, because a door frame does just that: frames that last moment for a few seconds. You can use the technique by pausing just before you start and just after you close your presentation.

- **Eye contact.** Look up and out. Making eye contact is one of the key elements of confident presentation. Move your head and eyes to take in the whole audience even if you can't actually catch anyone's eye individually. Make use of the 'Ms and Ws' technique: let your eye rove from the front to the back and from the back to the front taking in different parts of the audience as you speak. Two to three seconds is plenty of time for each person to feel included. If you can't bring yourself to look directly into their eyes, try focusing on the area around the eyebrows and nose.

- **Change seats.** A whole-body movement can change the mood, pace or focus of a presentation. If the presentation is going on a bit, the audience will get a different perspective, literally, if you change your seat. Also, you can avoid cramp by moving about, and fend off boredom through physical activity.

- **Mime.** Instead of speaking the word or phrase or concept, mime it.

- **Show how it's done.** Demonstrate the technique: show how you do it rather than just describe the actions. 'What should I do with my hands at an interview?' It's easier to show than describe.

- **Smile with your eyes as well as your mouth.** Try smiling with your eyes without moving your mouth; this will bring some expression to the eyes. Then smile properly. An open facial expression looks honest and friendly.

- **Eyebrow flash.** If you spot someone you know or made contact with before the presentation, then a quick flash of the eyebrows is a friendly acknowledgement and makes you appear confident.

- **Don't forget smell, touch and taste.**

FOCUS ON SMELL

- We have a primitive response to an aroma, an instant like or dislike. It might be evocative of the past or a particular person with pleasant or unpleasant associations, but it will take us on a journey somewhere.

- Use essential oils in advance of a presentation. For example, if your concentration is flagging, try a blend of rosemary, lemon and grapefruit to clear your head and give you a lift. Lavender and geranium can relax and refocus you and help you to communicate more effectively.

- To wake people up a bit or if the room is a bit stuffy, pass round peppermint oil on a piece of card, a peppermint sweet or peppermint teabag, or try that old-fashioned remedy for fainting: smelling salts. That will give them a shock to the system!

- Can you hire people for how they smell? Collect some free samples of after-shave and perfume from perfume counters or women's magazines. Write to the manufacturer and explain that you are conducting some research and ask for samples. Spray or dot the fragrance on to blotting paper or card. Business cards are about the right weight for this exercise. Pass them round and note people's response to the different smells.

- Use smell as a non-verbal introduction instead of a handshake. Give volunteers a brown paper bag each containing something that has a distinctive aroma: dried chrysanthemum heads, menthol crystals, coffee, for example. They approach each other and hold out the bag for the other to sniff – observe their reactions!

● Smell can be a repellent. Musty, damp stale smells, or the smell of stale food, body odour, bad food or drains, is a turn-off. If you can't get rid of it, you might be able to mask a repellent with an attractant.

● As an attractant, you could open the window to allow the smell of freshly cut grass to drift in, or that of freshly brewed coffee, vanilla, lavender furniture polish, sea breeze (ozone). Or find a way to set up one of these smells yourself.

● French beeswax has a divine smell. A small amount rubbed on a radiator will discreetly perfume a room.

'For the sense of smell, almost more than any other, has the power to recall memories and it is a pity that you use it so little.'
(Rachel Carson, biologist)

Get the audience to 'do it', not 'imagine it'. Suppose you were presenting material about pain or disability; then imagine the power of providing a fresh perspective, a different angle, by giving people an opportunity to experience it for themselves. Ask for volunteers if it is a large group or invite everyone to join in if it's a small group.

– Sight problems: smear washing-up liquid on spectacles and invite volunteers to read their notes.

– Hearing difficulties: have the volunteers insert soft foam earplugs, then listen to the remainder of the discussion with the plugs in place.

– Constant pain: have volunteers put pebbles, sweets or gravel in their shoes and then walk to the loo and back.

Use your body to be a better presenter

1. Walk like a winner.

2. Stand up to speak.

3. 'Plant' yourself in front of the audience.

4. Use the 'Hollywood pause'.

5. Own the stage.

6. Make eye contact with everyone in the audience at some time during the presentation.

7. Be aware of what you are doing with your hands.

8. Balance movement with stillness.

PHYSICAL WARM-UP BEFORE A PRESENTATION

Choose any or all of these:

- Stamp your feet, shake your fingers out, clench and unclench your hands, hit something hard or jump up and down to release some of the adrenaline and leave you calmer.

- Massage your neck muscles if they've tensed up. Place your little fingers on each side of your jaw under your ear lobes. Let your fingers find your neck muscles, spread your fingers apart and pull them downwards, gently dragging the skin. Repeat three times. This is good for relaxing the muscles a bit and improving your posture.

- Close your eyes and put one hand to rest lightly on your collarbone.

Breathe in, then breathe out counting down from 10 to 1, tapping your collarbone gently at each count. This is good for focusing and calming.

● If the thought of standing up to speak is terrifying you, why not start speaking sitting down. Stand up when you're ready or when you reach a point at which you need to access a flip chart or switch on a piece of equipment.

11 Language

In modern Western culture the majority of us can read and write up to a minimal standard and we admire those with a high level of language ability. We give linguistic ability high ranking in our society, along with digital intelligence and logical reasoning. The verbal presenter has the potential to entertain the audience with a large vocabulary and fluent delivery.

Are you a 'language' person?	YES	NO	SOMETIMES
1. Do you enjoy making puns, playing with words? Do you like poetry, fiction, biographies?			
2. Are you someone who reads anything and everything: backs of cereal packets, books, newspapers, magazines?			
3. Do you like crosswords, word puzzles and word games, Scrabble?			
4. Are you confident that you can express yourself in writing and when you talk?			
5. Can you give clear directions and instructions?			
6. Are you a good speller?			
7. Have you got an excellent vocabulary and do you enjoy finding just the right word or phrase?			
8. Are you someone who can debate and argue your point?			
9. Do you enjoy looking up words in a dictionary or thesarus?			
10. Do you like going to lectures or listening to tapes and can you easily absorb information by listening?			
TOTALS			

Dip into these ideas. Find something serendipitous you haven't tried before and make it work for you.

Adjectives, adverbs and verbs

Discover the joy (bliss, delight, pleasure, rapture, satisfaction) of taking your time to find just the right word.

Alliteration

For example, Vanilla Vanessa for someone who loves ice cream; Ten Top Tips.

Anecdote

Tell an illustrative story, an amusing story, a yarn (see Chapter 13 for how to tell a story).

Ask a question

Ask a question to which you do not expect the audience to respond – for example, 'What have an art school in Germany between the wars and colour consultants got in common?' (The answer is that it was at the Bauhaus that the seasonal theory of colour analysis was put forward.)

Catchphrase

You could use your own or one that you've made your own, your boss's or a celebrity's:

- 'er indoors.
- She who must be obeyed.
- Just do it.
- Come on down.
- You are the weakest link.
- Can I ask the audience?
- Beam me up, Scottie.
- Education, Education, Education.

Colloquialisms

Use colloquialisms carefully, eg 'Find your feet', 'In a jiffy'. Colloquialisms belong with an informal style and can add colour and life to any presentation; they add spice to a formal presentation.

Thesaurus

Consult the thesaurus for an alternative word. If we look up 'consult' we get: check, deliberate, discuss, confer, ask advice. Looking up 'alternative' gives us: option, choice. So, the first sentence of this sub-section might be rewritten as 'Check the thesaurus for a choice of words.'

Contrast

Add drama by using the contrast of intellectual versus emotional argument, personal evidence versus academic research.

Lt Col Martin Bricknell was talking about setting up an Army field hospital in Oman to support a military exercise in 2001. His introduction used the image versus reality contrast. The image was his verbal description, a word picture of the images that were conjured up in his mind's eye from the word 'Oman' – Arabian nights, palm trees, soft skies. The reality, as he showed us in a colour slide, was a vast, dirty, flat, sandpit with the odd bare tree.

Construction

Constructing messages so that people listen means including 'you' and 'your' more than 'I' and 'we' and making sure you've covered the WIIFM factor (What's In It For Me).

Dictionary definitions

Look up the meaning(s) of key words in the title of your presentation. For instance, if the title is 'The Importance of Networking in Modern Business Life', you would find that 'networking' is 'a system or procedure for catching or entrapping a person or persons' (*Concise Oxford Dictionary*) or that 'network' means 'an interconnected or interrelated chain, group, or system' (*Webster's New Collegiate Dictionary*).

Unusual dictionaries

Use dictionaries of quotations, slang, rhyming words, etc.

Dictionary dive

Let the dictionary fall open at any page and dive in with your finger. Whatever word your finger lands on, challenge yourself to use it somewhere in the presentation.

Find your own voice

Know your material so well that you can talk normally and concentrate on connecting with the audience.

Foreign words or phrases

If you speak other languages, then sprinkling your presentation with the occasional apposite word or phrase can be quite entertaining. When I was a child I learnt to speak Welsh, and I can still recall one or two words and phrases which I use to add piquancy to an otherwise formal presentation. If you know you have people in the audience from other countries, then including a greeting or well-known saying in their language can go some way to creating rapport. More than the odd word or phrase can grate, however, if your accent is not good.

'Funny stories' file

One of the best sources of funny stories is your own personal experience. Develop a 'funny stories' file. Brainstorm some memories, looking for stories, anecdotes or situations that can be used as examples around the key points in your presentation. Ask yourself:

- 'Have my children or grandchildren said anything recently that could be connected to this topic?'

- 'Have I had any embarrassing moments related to this point?'
- 'Has anyone I know had any embarrassing moments related to this subject?'

Jargon

Have fun with the latest buzzwords. Raise your game in the jargon ping-pong stakes. Use the jargon identifier. Select a word from each of the three columns for an intelligent-sounding technical term:

COLUMN 1	COLUMN 2	COLUMN 3
1. interactive	1. transitional	1. involvement
2. standardized	2. policy	2. capability
3. integrated	3. incremental	3. contingency
4. synchronized	4. monitoring	4. logic
5. parallel	5. time-phased	5. programming
6. automated	6. third-generation	6. architecture
7. visionary	7. reciprocal	7. feedback
8. flexible	8. state-of-the-art	8. training
9. revolutionary	9. phased	9. availability

Metaphor and analogy

A metaphor is 'the application of a name or descriptive term or phrase to an object or action that is imaginatively but not literally applicable, where there is a correspondence or partial similarity':

The future is an open sea where you can sail in any direction.

The rosy apple of our life was browning over.

What metaphor would you use to describe:

- a series of unexpected windfalls;

- a run of bad luck;

- a very untidy office;

- a dull and cloudy day;

- a situation where there were no alternatives.

Simile

A simile is 'a figure of speech involving the comparison of one thing with another of a different kind as an illustration or ornament (eg brave as a lion), drawing a parallel'.

> **'You look just the same,' we say to each other, but of course we are eerily different, like four schoolgirls who've been left in the microwave too long.'**
> *(Kate Muir, writing in* The Times on Saturday *about her school reunion)*

Parables and stories

Use a parable, folk tale, story or legend. Asking, 'What do you want out of your career' could lead to asking, 'What is your heart's desire?', which could lead to *The Wizard of Oz*, which could lead you to:

- Follow the Yellow Brick Road.

- Face up to your fears.

- Identify what you need. The Lion wanted courage, the Tin Man wanted a heart and the Straw Man wanted a brain.

Misquote

For example: 'The lady's not for turning' (Margaret Thatcher) instead of 'The lady's not for burning' (Christopher Fry); 'And so to bid perchance to scream' (a novice going to an auction of memorabilia), instead of 'And so to bed perchance to dream' (Shakespeare, *Hamlet*).

Mnemonics

Mnemonics are memorization techniques that help you or your audience make a connected sequence out of an unconnected one. For example:

- in musical notation, notes on the treble stave, EGBDF: 'Every Good Boy Deserves Fun';
- the colours of the rainbow, red, orange, yellow, green, blue, indigo, violet: 'Read Out Your Green Book In Verse';
- number of days in the month:

  Thirty days hath September,

  April, June and dull November

  All the rest have thirty-one,

  Excepting February clear,

  Which has twenty-eight

  And twenty-nine each leap year.

THE DAFFY
For opening and closing a presentation
Demand Attention, Finish with a Flourish, Yes!!

Motto

A motto is a maxim adopted as a rule of conduct. Also called a saying, a slogan, a byword, an aphorism. For example: 'Do as you would be done by' or 'any excuse for a party.'

Onomatopoeia

Onomatopoeia is the formation of a word from a sound associated with what is named (eg cuckoo, sizzle, hiss, tick). It is useful to add to rather dull material.

Palindrome

A palindrome is a word or phrase that reads the same backwards as forwards, eg rotator, nurses run.

Play with words

You could say key words backwards, eg Prince Charming: Prince Mingchar.

Or you could invent a nickname, eg St Anthony for Tony Blair, or Golden Boots for David Beckham, or The Blonde Bombsite (instead of 'blonde bombshell'), or Sic transit Gloria Swanson (instead of 'sic transit gloria mundi').

'Printspeak'

'Printspeak' is the affliction of writing for the eye and not the ear; it comes out like a foreign language. Avoid it at all costs when preparing a presentation. Always check your writing for printspeak by reading it aloud.

Quotations

Keep a quotations file. Make a note of anything current or historical that takes your fancy. Perennial favourites include:

- Shakespeare;
- Chinese proverbs;
- poetry;
- song lyrics;
- the Bible;
- the Koran;
- your favourite author or book, or professional journal;

- horoscopes;
- nursery rhymes.

Quote from famous speeches, today's newspaper, reviews, articles, the most recent play, book, film or scandal. There are many Web sites devoted to recent and historical speeches. Some have soundbites as well.

Repetition

Don't be afraid – fear not – to say the same thing – *la même chose* – in different ways to be sure to get your message across.

Scripts

When working with a script written by someone else, particularly if it's not very good, or not going down well, for goodness sake go off-script now and again. Use passion, conviction and humour and get some eye contact going.

Slang

Using slang can be a useful and colourful way to warm up a formal style or add occasional spice to an informal style.

'Stump speech'

A 'stump speech' is a well-worn presentation, tried and tested in many situations with a variety of audiences. It is something that can be recycled, freshened up, made topical for each new situation by adding local references and personalizing the material. It is a presentation that you are so comfortable with you can deliver it at any time; it fits you and suits you and makes you look good – just like a perfect little black dress, or favourite jacket.

Trawl widely

Trawl widely to make your presentation as interesting as possible:

- from poetry to politics;
- from football to science fiction;
- from fashion to fiction;
- from history to geography;
- from the evident to the obscure.

Word pictures

We all have the ability to create our very own 'special effects department' in our head, and we enjoy listening to someone who can create word pictures for us. 'The pictures are better on radio.'

Warning

A verbal presentation is not a good vehicle for getting across complex ideas. Simplify and refine constantly.

DEVELOP YOUR WORD POWER

Tick the words you know:

1. capricious	11. molledize	21. curtilage	31. subjective
2. tepid	12. yolk	22. fuliginous	32. abrasive
3. ullifont	13. exclude	23. negrity	33. mefficent
4. turbulent	14. yerdic	24. primeval	34. preface
5. varminous	15. gentian	25. sullein	35. gryony
6. mongrel	16. larboard	26. infeasible	36. lassitude
7. polyphagous	17. horomene	27. pungent	37. clasure
8. aphid	18. preferment	28. spole	38. autodidactic
9. warped	19. filcrum	29. vouchers	39. inherently
10. oscitution	20. currish	30. furtive	40. antipodes

Score one point for every word you ticked

If you ticked any of the words below, take off two points for each word:

3   5   10   11   14   17   19

23   25   28   33   35   37

(With thanks to Terry Doyle and Paul Meara, authors of the BBC publi-cation *li´ngô! – How to Learn a Language*, who gave me the inspiration for this exercise.)

George Orwell, in *Plain English*, set out the following rules:

1. Never use a long word where a short one would do.

2. If it is possible to cut out a word, cut it out.

3. Never use the passive when you can use the active.

4. Never use a foreign phrase, a scientific word or a jargon word if you can think of an everyday English equivalent.

'Speech is not a row of words, it is a kaleidoscope.'

(Anon)

12 Pictures

Human beings are visually dominant and use this sense above all others to make sense of the world. Some of us are also predominantly visually intelligent and we seek and process information visually. Either we need to 'see' something physically or we will create pictures in our 'mind's eye'. The world is full of visual images, and we can study the meaning of what we see through semiology: the general (if tentative) science of signs and symbols. We are surrounded by myriad ways in which human beings, individually or in groups, communicate or attempt to communicate visually: gestures, advertisements, language itself, food, objects, music, clothes and many other things. When you are designing a presentation, its visual elements will be your opportunity to underscore other messages in other channels as well as being messages in themselves.

Are you a 'visual' person?		YES	NO	SOMETIMES
1.	Do you have a good sense of colour and can you make successful colour schemes?			
2.	Do you like to make a visual record of events, family gatherings, holidays etc by taking photos, using a camcorder or making drawings?			
3.	Can you draw something fairly accurately?			
4.	Do you dress stylishly?			
5.	Are you a great people watcher?			
6.	Do you 'show' people what you mean using your hands or by making drawings or diagrams?			
7.	Do you enjoy jigsaw puzzles, word puzzles and mazes?			
8.	Are you a good speller and can you remember words by sight?			
9.	Do you doodle when listening, making notes or thinking about something?			
10.	Do you like to read rather than be read to?			
	TOTALS			

Dip into the following ideas. Find something serendipitous you haven't tried before and make it work for you.

- **Use colour to distinguish between similar elements.** If I was explaining to an audience that 'My BEST Communication Style' had four distinct styles, I could allocate a colour for each style: B = red, E = yellow, S = green and T = blue, and wear an appropriately coloured hat in turn as I mentioned them. Or I could use four pieces of A4 paper or large cards in each of the colours and hold up the matching card.

- **Develop visual symbols for taking notes.** Encourage your audience to do the same using colour coding, stars, squares, arrows, squiggles to emphasize or add logic or meaning to the notes.

- **Use an image to represent a key word.** You can emphasize a word with a well-chosen image and to bring freshness to a cliché:

  - 'Piece of cake'. When you know something's going to be really easy.

  - 'A matter of perception'. People see the same thing differently. Do you see two heads in profile or a castle, a chess piece?

  - 'Rich mixture'. What might you use when you want to suggest a dense combination of good things – this could refer to people, ideas or activities – a Christmas pudding?

  - 'Making the difference'. Maybe a photo of David Beckham, who always makes a difference when he goes on the pitch and doesn't just go through the motions.

- **Use an object to represent a key word, concept or commonly used phrase** to emphasize it or bring originality to it:

Table 12.1   Use of objects as illustration

Concept	Object that could be used
TLC (tender loving care)	Yellowing plant or wilting seedling
Energize	Can of sports drink, eg Red Bull, Lucozade
Clarify, see more clearly	Pair of glasses or binoculars
Focus on	Magnifying glass
Reflect on	Mirror
Sell	Banknotes, coins, wallet, purse
Take you on a journey	Travel card, flight ticket, map, compass
New direction	Pointer, compass, arrow
Enjoy yourselves, have fun	Balloons, partypoppers, squeakers, funny nose, party hat
Guidelines	Coloured tape on the floor
Transform, change	Magic trick
Create a little magic	Magic wand, stardust, magic trick
Wearing a different hat	Hat, cap, party hat, uniform hat or cap

Dr Jonas Ridderstråle, Assistant Professor for Advanced Studies in Leadership at Stockholm School of Economics, illustrated his message to human resources (HR) directors about excelling in E(motional)-business with Viagra in one hand and Prozac in the other. Casually dressed, with huge energy he strode around the stage with no notes – an easy performance born out of much experience.

- **Use a single object to represent a concept.** Place the object in front of you where everyone can see it and ask your audience to think what it might represent. You can ask them to think about their response in silence or you can invite them to call out their responses, or suggest a minute to think then get them to call out their suggestions. Someone is always willing to start the ball rolling. You'll probably get the answer you want, but if not, you can provide it when you are ready to start. What connections would you make with the following objects?

- a single rose;

- bubbles;

- a candle;

- a whistle;

- soap.

● **Use an object or image to mark the occasion or place:**

- saint's days: vase of daffodils on St David's Day, a green theme for St Patrick's;

- festivals: Diwali, Hanukkah, Notting Hill Carnival, Gay Pride, Halloween;

- holidays: Bank Holidays, Christmas, Easter;

- anniversaries: birth, death, discovery, invention;

- links to the area, the location, venue, people in the audience or the organization and its business, eg a birthday of someone in the audience.

- **Use cartoons.** Find something relevant to the point that just lightens the mood (get permission to use it).

"The author wants to see the cover before we print it!"

Cartoon © Douglas Hall, 1995

- **Collect a picture file.** Look in newspapers, magazines, free advertising fliers. File under different headings for ease of retrieval:

  - people;

  - places;

  - objects;

  - pictures representing abstract concepts.

One of the high street banks was using a gerbera (a large daisy-like flower that comes in a variety of bright colours) in one of its advertising campaigns. The size, shape and colour of the image were just right to represent something that was a perfect shape – in this case, a perfect career in the bank.

- **Use photos of real people and events**, past or present. I sometimes use as an introductory slide a single photo or a collage of me, or my mother or grandmother and my daughter – four generations of women in teaching and training.

- **Use drawings.** Original drawings have an immediacy and freshness if the audience has been used to a diet of clip art.

- **Use postcards.** Picturesque scenes, historic sights, unusual objects can all contribute to the story, message or theme you are constructing.

- **Use visual logic.** When you are designing a slide presentation using PowerPoint or acetates you can engage your audience by indirect means using a logical visual flow to the look of your slides. Your audience won't necessarily know what's going on but they will want to see what comes next. Some examples:

  - progression of light to dark of same colour, dark to light, light to shadow;

  - progression of colours through the rainbow, using different colours for each part of the talk;

  - progression of size of an object – getting larger or smaller;

  - pieces that go together to form a whole, eg instruments in a band, a jigsaw puzzle, the Beatles;

  - numerical progression;

  - alphabetical progression;

  - chronological progression;

  - progression through the seasons of the year.

- **Use a 3D model of the idea or concept.** Both in the architectural and in the metaphorical sense, a 3D model will get attention. For example, there is a popular toddler's toy on the market, a large rigid plastic ball where you have to match the shapes of objects to the cut-out shapes in the ball and to post the objects into the ball. A good way to illustrate the concept of a perfect fit in a partnership, a business, a new appointment.

- **Use samples.** If you have written a book, a paper or a report or if you have a product or process to discuss, then at the very least you should have a sample with you. If you have an idea for a new shape of coffee mug you would mock it up so people could see it.

- **Use a demonstration of the technique or idea.** If you were talking about destressing breathing techniques, you would demonstrate the technique rather than describe it, so that everyone could see how your body was behaving.

- **Use a visual link:**

  - shapes;

  - animals;

  - flowers;

  - colours;

  - precious stones;

  - minerals;

  - elements.

- **Use your image and style to enhance your message.** Dress up a little more than the audience expects. Use what you wear to enhance your status, your presentation role and your communication style. Decide whether you should appear smart, scruffy, stylish, colourful, neutral, glamorous, sexy, conventional, sporty, weird.

- **Use the power of colour in what you wear.** High contrasts such as navy and white, black and cream attract attention and symbolize authority; warm colours advance and are friendly; cool colours recede and are more formal.

- **Use your accessories.** You can make a subtle or overt reference to your topic or show allegiance to a cause via your choice of tie. I've seen speakers wearing a range from horrendous to achingly chic, including Garrick Club tie, old school ties, ties with foxes, teddy bears or Father Christmas, National Trust tie, hand-painted water-colour ties, Institute of Directors tie and a tie from the speaker's local choir. Cufflinks can do a similar job. I've seen all these on presenters' cuffs:

– Hot and cold taps – energy? New housing stock?

– Trees – sustainable resources? Growth? Gardening?

– Symbols for male and female – equal opportunities? the gender gap? the glass ceiling?

– Dollar or pound signs – gambling? Financial implications? The Budget? Exchange rates?

– Bride and groom – wedding speech? The current divorce rate?

– Pigs – male chauvinism? The impossible might happen?

● **Use a brooch or pin.** This can be a way of making a subtle or overt reference to your topic or of showing allegiance to a cause, not just a fashion statement. For example, you could use a brooch or pin representing one of the following:

– mammals, birds, insects;

– Aids, breast cancer;

– book (for an author);

– scissors (for a craftsperson);

– laptop (for an IT specialist);

– palette (for an art topic);

– an Elvis pin (for a cultural history topic).

- **Use clip art.** Don't just rely on what came with your desktop package but trawl widely for a range of visual images. There are wonderful examples you can download direct from the Internet, or buy into sophisticated packages.

- **Use visual drama.** Make your entrance into a darkened room.

- **Wear a mask.** Masks are available from joke shops, fancy dress shops, museum shops.

PART III

Cut out and keep

13 Recipes

Putting a presentation together is rather like cooking a meal. When you're very busy or when you don't feel the slightest bit creative and haven't got an idea in your head, it's really useful to have a tried and trusted recipe to hand. So, when you have a presentation coming up, you might ask yourself:

- **What ingredients do I need?**

    - Style and impact: Do I need warmth, sincerity, persuasiveness, to state the facts, help the audience to anticipate what's to come or calm down after a hectic session, wake them up after lunch; do I need to be relaxed, formal, powerful?

    - Clothes: What will I need to wear? Shall I put a jacket on, my best suit or just freshen up a bit?

– Body language: Would it be a good idea to stand up, sit down, lean on the desk, move about, stay still, sit on the floor?

● **What have I already got in stock?** Have I got something similar I've done before? A sound structure, an appropriate quote, a successful story, some good slides?

● **How long have I got?** How long should you take? A well-prepared short presentation is better than a long waffly one. Most of the suggestions listed below aim to deliver your message in a couple of minutes. Recipe no 6 is designed for a 10-minute presentation. If you have to do a longer presentation, then divide it up into manageable chunks using the same method. A 30-minute presentation then becomes three 10-minute presentations. and if you use the 10-minute recipe you will get a pleasing flow and shape to the presentation and retain your audience's attention. The only difference is that you would save your punchline or dramatic close until the very end.

Because we speak at a rate of about 120–150 words per minute, keep this guide handy when you are at the planning and preparation stage.

1,250 written words = approx 10 minutes spoken
250 written words = approx 2 minutes spoken

SIX PRESENTATION RECIPES THAT REALLY WORK

Whatever the circumstances, you will need:

● one basic structure (beginning, middle and end or introduction, body and conclusion);

- one key message;
- two or three main points.

Add according to taste:

- a prop or attention-grabber;
- a way of involving your audience.

RECIPE 1: INTRODUCING A SPEAKER

1. Well known for… or with a reputation for…
2. Current position.
3. Brief career history.
4. Say the speaker's name.
5. Personal qualities.
6. Set of values.
7. Personal anecdote.
8. The subject for today is…
9. Please welcome… (name).

What ingredients do I need?

State the speaker's credentials and make the audience anticipate the benefits of the presentation. Use an upbeat tone.

How long have I got?

One and a half to two minutes.

'This morning I'd like to introduce a man with a remarkable reputation as an advocate – an advocate for patients' rights. He is currently advising three local hospitals on best practice around stakeholder involvement. Following an early career in the motor industry where he was responsible for implementing industry standards in Investors in People, he made an important career move into health care. He is of course Andrew Beasley. He is a man of great charm and commitment about whom the phrase "an iron hand in a velvet glove" could have been created. He believes passionately in making sure that the voices of those least able to make themselves heard are heard. I remember many occasions, as I'm sure you all do, when Andrew simply refused to take no for an answer. I'm delighted he can be with us today, and his subject "Patient Involvement – How to Get to Yes" is one close to our hearts in this department. He has designed a 20-minute presentation and will be happy to take questions at the end. Please welcome… Andrew Beasley.'
(180 words)

Confidence card

Key phrases written on a 10.5 cm × 14.5 cm index card.

ANDREW BEASLEY
Speaker no 3, 10.40 am

- Advocate for Patients' Rights
- Best practice, Stakeholder Involvement
- Motor industry >> health care
- ANDREW BEASLEY
- iron hand in velvet glove
- make voices heard
- won't take no for an answer
- Patient Involvement – how to get to YES

15 mins, questions afterwards

RECIPE 2: SAYING GOODBYE TO A COLLEAGUE WHO IS RETIRING

1. State the occasion and the person's name.

2. The person's history.

3. Personal anecdote.

4. Good qualities.

5. More time for...

6. Good wishes for the future.
7. Raise your glasses to… (say name).

What ingredients do I need?

The personal touch: say the person's name frequently, reiterate the purpose of the gathering. Get the facts right, both personal and professional. The order of the points is not as important as getting them all in and getting the names, dates and places correct.

How long have I got?

Two to three minutes.

'Today is a special day. It's also a sad day because we are saying goodbye to Gwen Jones. Gwen is retiring after 18 years with A, B & C Pharmaceuticals. Gwen started here in 1985 as a clerk in the Supplies Department at our Brentwood site. She then became section head and went on to become Office Manager in 1997. Those of you who were here in 1999 will remember the move from Brentwood to Isleworth and the way Gwen managed to get us all here – plus Amanda's beloved potted plant! A typical Gwen touch was the coffee mugs. Never being known to miss out on a free gift, our Gwen charmed the catering suppliers into giving us not six but 24 new mugs printed with our logo.

We will remember Gwen for her efficiency, her calmness in a crisis and her cheerful good humour. She is leaving us today, and after a holiday in Bali with her husband, Clive, she intends to divide her time between her other two loves: her garden and her grandchildren, Simon and Becky. Our good wishes go with you, Gwen, for the next stage in your life. We'd like to present you with this cheque, which comes with our very good wishes. In the words of your favourite Beatles number: "If there's anything that you want, if there's anything we can do, just call on us and we'll send it along..." Ladies and gentlemen, friends and colleagues, please raise your glasses to... Gwen.' (250 words)

Confidence card

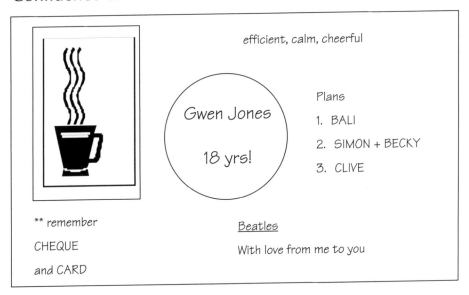

RECIPE 3: A GENERAL INTRODUCTION TO A PRESENTATION

1. Say hello and state your name (if the audience doesn't know you) and your role if it has not been clearly stated already.

2. Create an impact; catch the attention of the audience (see Chapters 9–12 for some ideas).

3. State the theme of your topic.

4. State your credentials – not your autobiography, but a few choice items from your CV that are relevant to the audience and to the topic.

5. Explain the aim of the presentation.

6. Emphasize the benefits of the presentation.

7. Describe the features of the presentation. Give the audience a map. Indicate the structure and timing of your presentation, the main topics to be covered and how you will be handling questions.

8. Get on with it!

What ingredients do I need?

Clarity of aim and purpose, and a clear outcome for the audience.

How long have I got?

One and a half to two minutes.

'Hello, I'm Miranda Green and I'm a career consultant. This means that I help people to enjoy their working lives by helping them to plan their career progression. I also write about careers, and my session is based on my latest book, which is called *Perfect Career Paths*.

'In this session I intend to give you some tools and techniques to support you in the next stage of your career journey – to help you iden-tify what you really want and where you want to be.

'The session is in three parts and takes the form of three questions:

1. What makes a job fulfilling?

2. How do you get yourself promoted?

3. How do you become an effective networker?

Each question will have:

1. some input from me;

2. an exercise for you to do on your own;

3. an opportunity for you discuss the issues with other people.

'We have 40 minutes for the whole session and I will use this musical signal to let you know when your thinking time is up and when group discussion time is up. So that's 10 minutes for each of the three parts plus 10 minutes at the end for questions, but I'll also be happy to take questions and other contributions throughout the session.

'Let's start by talking about work–life balance.' (221 words)

Five-card trick

The five cards are: one each for the Introduction and Conclusion plus three cards for your three main points. This is a very adaptable recipe and particularly useful if you don't have much time to prepare. Any small cards or Post-it notes will do.

RECIPE 4: SAYING THANK YOU FOR AN AWARD

What ingredients do I need?

Brevity, sincerity and a light touch. If you can't be amusing, be brief and sincere.

How long have I got?

One minute or less.

1. Compose yourself if you have become emotional.
2. Say what it's for (an award? a gift?) and why you are pleased to receive it.
3. Say thank you, both to the people who gave it to you (name(s)) and to the people who helped you (names and contribution).
4. Special thanks (their names and a personal message to them).
5. Get off.

RECIPE 5: TELLING A STORY

What ingredients do I need?

The structure of a good story.

1. When.
2. Where.

3. Who.

4. What's the context?

5. What happened?

6. What had to be done?

7. What went wrong?

8. How was it put right?

9. How did it end?

How long have I got?

Two to four minutes.

Once upon a time: the Cinderella story

When	Background, when it happened	Once upon a time, a long time ago
Where	Location	In a far off land, in a big castle on top of a hill
Who	The players, who was involved	A rich old man, recently widowed, lives with his only daughter Cinderella, who is as beautiful as she is kind
What's the context	What kind of situation it is, the context in which its happening	He is very lonely and decides to get married again, this time to a widow with two daughters who are very ugly and unkind
What happened?	State the problem or challenge for example, a major difficulty to overcome, a task to be fulfilled, a deception, a dragon to be slain	Cinderella's new stepmother and her stepsisters treat her cruelly, banishing her to the kitchen to live like a servant. They squander her father's fortune on expensive clothes and extravagant parties making him unhappy and blind to Cinderella's situation. The ugly sisters won't let Cinderella go to Prince Charming's Grand Ball, so there's no opportunity for her to meet a husband and escape from her situation
What had to be done	What was needed to change the situation, solve the problem? Resources used? money, effort, people, magic, wit, wisdom	Fairy Godmother transforms the pumpkin into a coach, the rats and mice into horses and footmen, and Cinderella's rags into a ball gown, so that she can go to the ball
What went wrong?	Drama	Cinderella goes to the ball and Prince Charming falls in love with her. The clock strikes midnight, the magic will stop at the last stroke. Cinderella runs out into the night before the Prince can stop her. In her hurry, she drops one of her glass slippers
How was it put right?	How the situation was resolved. Happily, unhappily, money saved, reputation intact	Because he wants so much to meet her again, Prince Charming ensures that every young woman in the land is visited so that, regardless of rank, each one can try on the glass slipper to see if it fits. When it fits, he knows he's found Cinderella
How did it end?	The result	Using this device, Prince Charming finds Cinderella, they get married and live happily every after

'I keep six honest serving men,
They taught me all I knew,
Their names are What and Why and When,
And How and Where and Who.'
(Rudyard Kipling, 'The Elephant's Child')

RECIPE 6: SURE-FIRE FORMAT FOR A SHORT (10-MINUTE) PRESENTATION

What ingredients do I need?

An element of formality, clarity, to reach a wide range of people in the audience.

How long have I got?

Ten minutes maximum.

Presentation to new graduates about interview techniques

	TIME	TOPIC	ILLUSTRATION
Entrance and opening remarks	½ minute	Get that Job!	Ask challenging question, today's newspaper
Introduction	1¼ minutes	See intro slide for sequence	OHP slide, verbal + text map of presentation
Topic A: point 1	1 minute		OHP slide cartoon
point 2	1½ minutes		Talk, describe recent research
Topic B: point 1	1½ minutes		Talk, tell personal anecdote or story
point 2	½ minute		Demonstrate, show how to do it
Topic C: point 1	1 minute		OHP slide, pie chart
point 2	1 minute		Ask audience to make a list
Summary	1½ minutes		OHP text, list of action points
Punchline and exit	¼ minute		Quote from professional journal, pop song
TOTAL	**10 minutes**		

RECIPES FOR EXITS AND ENTRANCES

Ideas for opening a presentation

Analogy

Making a presentation about making a presentation is like being trapped in a hall of mirrors. Trying to see what you are doing while you are doing it, is to experience the extremes of distortion and flattery. The medium is undoubtedly the message in this situation.

Anecdote

Relate an incident or story about yourself, your team, your family. This is not the same as a story, because it is about real events.

Casual start

'Melanie and I were discussing as we came up in the lift the issue of de-layering.' At least one person is on your side, and you have made a start without appearing to make a speech. Your 'real' introduction comes after the casual start. It doesn't much matter what you say here as long as it's relaxed and friendly, because the purpose of this kind of opening is to let your audience become accustomed to how you look and how you sound before you begin your presentation proper.

Compliment the audience

Paying the audience a genuine compliment about their success, their creativity, their hospitality is a warm way to open the proceedings.

Empathetic opening

'If I were sitting in your place now I might be expecting to be bored or lectured at, expecting just another progress report. Today I've got something different for you...' This is a good way of getting rid of preconceived ideas and getting audience involvement. It doesn't matter whether they agree with you or not – you can go on to state your case.

Historical

Something about the history of your topic can be an excellent way of getting started. It doesn't matter too much how you structure it, because it's a device to help you focus and get started and to help the audience position what you have to say. A brief glimpse of the past can be effective, but don't get involved in a historical survey. Keep it short and strictly relevant.

Local colour

If you are speaking away from your usual base, then it is polite to say something warm about the locale. You may hate the place, but people do have to work there. You can find something pleasant to say about almost anywhere. 'I never fail to be impressed by the gardens here at this time of year.' Local colour has to be sincere to work; if it's an obvious bit of smarm, it deserves to fail.

Mind-reading

'I think I know what many of you are anticipating at this stage of the proceedings. Yes, you're right: we're going to look at last week's bed management figures.' A little 'swirl' goes through the audience as they try to keep up, and you have their attention for the next part of the presentation.

Once upon a time

Tell a story that has humour, is topical and has an intriguing twist. To be successful, your story has to be relevant to the topic not just a funny story for its own sake. Keep it short, personal or personalized, and well told. If the story is against yourself, so much the better. The ability to laugh at yourself wins over an audience even if you are not a gifted teller of tales. The story should be short and to the point, with names, dates, references, places and punchlines clearly recalled, not fumbled for. Do not attempt anything dramatic or powerful or comic unless 1) you are a naturally gifted storyteller, or 2) it actually happened to you.

Pose a question

'Do you believe that our globalization strategy should expand or consolidate at this stage?' The audience instinctively tries to arrive at an answer and you have their attention. At an internal conference I heard the Managing Director get instant attention by asking, 'How many of you think that allocating new budget to management development is a waste of time?'

Quotation

To quote from a well-known person or author works best if you have learnt the words by heart and can deliver them straight to the audience without using prompts. Among a rich array of resources are Shakespeare, the Bible, the Koran, Chinese philosophy, the 'this week's notable sayings' column in Sunday papers or gossip magazines, American presidents. They are all a never-ending source of good openers.

State the facts

'The number of active consultants increased in this quarter by 18 per cent. This exceeds our target by 6 per cent. If the trend continues at this rate, we will need to increase our support mechanisms exponentially.'

Shock

Not merely a stunt to open with, but shocking words. To the marketing department:

'Marketing is a waste of time and money'... pause for effect ... 'unless, of course, it is used properly as a business tool not an added extra.'

Surprise start

Making use of the unexpected is a good way to catch the audience's attention. Allow a few seconds for recovery from the effect of your stunt. The real introduction will follow your surprise. Match the surprise to the message. Play Gloria Gaynor singing 'I will survive' to a group of people thinking about giving up their safe jobs to become entrepreneurs. Tap dance, do a strip tease, play the violin, blow bubbles, play loud music, spray the air, turn all the lights off, run on, cartwheel on. Perform a magic trick. Juggle.

Surprising statistics

'One in five university undergraduates do not have the basic communication skills employers need' – an attention-grabbing way to start a talk to students about job opportunities.

Ideas for closing a presentation

Anecdote

An anecdote usually works best if it captures one of your presentation's key messages. The anecdote could be a cautionary tale or a success story. The key criterion is that it should be about real people and real situations.

Ask for action

If you want your audience to act, to do something as a result of your presentation, then ASK them. Make it clear what you want. If you want action now, not later, say so. Asking for action is a good way to start off a discussion if you want to have one. Ask for the sale. 'When you leave the lecture theatre today I'd like to ask those of you who don't already have their own copy to buy my latest book.'

Drama

Dramatic effects are essentially about contrast: loud/soft, dark/light/ sweet/sour. Using a deliberate dramatic device using sight, sound, movement or emotion can refocus the audience's attention, particularly if you use another sense to support the spoken word. A well thought out dramatic effect can be a wonderful way to leave the audience with a clear message. A big effect works best with a big audience; it can misfire in a small group, because you're too close together.

Fear

Use with care or you run the risk of alienating the audience, but an element of fear to promote action can occasionally be justified: for example, if you want your audience to take action to prevent crime, to be more aware of their personal safety, to safeguard their jobs or to minimize unwanted press attention.

Incentive

We all love a bargain. Can you offer a reward or incentive of some kind by way of closing your presentation? Invite people to pick up their copy of your notes from you in person, maybe?

Offer a choice

State the alternatives. In your summary, give greater weight (through vocal tone and body language) to the one you favour.

Pay a compliment

'It's been a marvellous occasion and I can't wait for the next time!'

Question and option

'It is now clear, ladies and gentlemen, what we must do. The question is, who is going to do it and how soon can we expect results?' Or, 'Shall we give up now or let the competition know we intend to fight? The choice is yours.'

Story

In the same way that a good story, well told, makes an excellent way to start a presentation, a good story, well told, is an equally good way to close a presentation. When used as the conclusion to a presentation, the story should be shorter than the opening story because once people know you are closing down, their attention can wander. The same rules apply as for the opening story: it should be short and to the point, with names, dates, references, places and punchlines clearly recalled, not fumbled for.

Summary

An impressive short review of the main messages can stand alone or be mixed with one of the other means of closing.

Surprise ending

Sometimes, memorability is a more important outcome than the message. Closing with a song would certainly help people remember you and not just the message.

Upbeat close

An inspiring or uplifting message is needed on some occasions. 'I've never been so certain in my life that we have the right people – courageous, strong and intelligent people – to take us on to the most challenging stage of our corporate development.'

PRESENTATION ESSENTIALS

Let us recall here an illustration that has already appeared in Chapter 1:

Coping with nerves	Creating interest
Building rapport with the audience	Handling questions with confidence

The four cornerstones self-checker

You might find it useful to make a note of any 'aha' moments.:

- Where did I start?
- What's become clear to me?
- Why is it meaningful for me?
- What tip have I picked up?
- How can I brand it with my personal style?
- When can I try it out?

1. It's OK to be yourself

2. 2 or 3 key points are all you need

3. Your audience is not the enemy

4. You don't have to be perfect to be successful

5. Humour helps

6. You can't avoid preparation

7. Take a whole brain approach

14 Checklists and formats

Presentation skills scorecard

YES		NO
YES	objectives stated	NO
YES	route map	NO
YES	logical flow	NO
YES	evidence of research	NO
YES	rapport with audience	NO
YES	use of equipment	NO
YES	use of support material	NO
YES	use of word pictures	NO
YES	pings, enhancers, sparklers	NO
YES	eye contact, smile	NO
YES	gesture, mannerisms, stance	NO
YES	tone, level of voice	NO
YES	clarity of speech	NO
YES	handling questions	NO
YES	confidence, nerves	NO
YES	accidents and emergencies	NO
YES	anything else	NO
Total		Total

Learning points:

Development areas:

Sure-fire timed format for making a 10-minute presentation

Audience:

Total time available:

The subject:

Desired outcome:

	TIME	TOPIC	ILLUSTRATION
Entrance and opening remarks	½ minute		
Introduction	1¼ minutes		
Topic A: point 1	1 minute		
point 2	1½ minutes		
Topic B: point 1	1½ minutes		
point 2	½ minute		
Topic C: point 1	1 minute		
point 2	1 minute		
Summary	1½ minutes		
Punchline and exit	¼ minute		
TOTAL	10 minutes		

'BE YOUR OWN ROADIE' CHECKLIST	
✔ CHECK ROLE	
✔ CHECK SCRIPT	
✔ CHECK PROPS AND STAGE MANAGEMENT	
✔ CHECK SOUND	
✔ CHECK LIGHTING	
✔ CHECK COSTUME	
✔ CHECK EQUIPMENT	
✔ REHEARSAL	
✔ WARM-UP	
✔ GET THE FEEL OF THE AUDIENCE	
✔ AMENITIES	
✔ REPAIR KIT	

MAKING A PRESENTATION
QUICK RETRIEVAL DATA BANK

Date	**Venue**
Time	**Contact**
Topic title	**What I'm not going to cover**
What I'm going to cover	
Audience profile	**Outcomes**
Size, gender, age range Specialist/generalist/mixed Anything special	Overt Covert
Key objectives	**Venue**
1. 2. 3.	Equipment Room size and type Furniture
Total time available	**Support:**
Start time Finish time Time allowed for questions	Technician Props Equipment Clothes
30-second version of my main message:	

BE YOUR OWN PRESENTATION SKILLS DOCTOR	
Objective questions	**Your responses**
1. When did you last do a presentation?	
2. Where did it take place?	
3. Who was there?	
4. What was it about?	
5. How many times before have you given this presentation?	
6. What evidence do you have of the success or otherwise of your performance?	
7. To what extent were your personal outcomes met?	
8. What was the main outcome?	
Subjective questions	**Your responses**
9. How did you feel – at the time? before? after?	
10. How did you do? What were your impressions?	
11. What feedback did you get?	
12. What went well?	
13. What went badly?'	
14. What would you change?	
15. As a result of previous presentations, what have you learnt about – yourself, audiences, presentations?	
16. What would you like to work on in order to improve?	

VOCAL IMPACT

Measure the VOCAL IMPACT of your presentations

TAKE POINTS OFF FOR	−2	−1		+1	+2	ADD ON POINTS FOR
Sounding wobbly or shaky						Sounding confident
Mumbling or talking through clenched teeth or tight mouth						Enunciating clearly through relaxed facial muscles, using lips and tongue
Getting out of breath						Breathing naturally
Using ums and errs						Using pauses effectively
Faltering, mispronouncing words						Pronouncing words clearly
Speaking softly						Using the volume dial
Not conveying feeling while speaking						Conveying feeling while speaking
Speaking in a monotone						Varying the 'colour' of your voice
Not emphasizing words that have a special meaning or emotion						Emphasizing important words
Galloping through your words						Speaking at a natural conversational pace

Getting squeaky or growly				Speaking at a natural, low to medium pitch
Not using pauses				Using pauses and allowing occasional silences
Anything else				Anything else
total −2s				total +2s
total −1s				total +1s
Your **VOCAL IMPACT** total score is:				

Take 2 points off if the observation on the left is **almost always** true for you.

Take 1 point off if the observation on the left is **occasionally** true for you.

Add 1 point if the observation on the right is **sometimes** true for you.

Add 2 points if the observation on the right is **almost always** true for you.

Add up your -2 and -1 scores for the left-hand column.

Add up your +2 and +1 scores for the right hand column.

Subtract the left-hand column score from the right-hand column score. The resulting score is your **VOCAL IMPACT** factor.

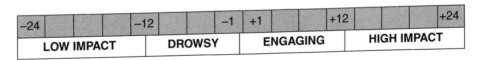

−24			−12			−1	+1			+12			+24
LOW IMPACT				**DROWSY**			**ENGAGING**			**HIGH IMPACT**			

SNOOZE-METER

Measure the SNOOZE factor of your presentations

TAKE POINTS OFF FOR	−2	−1		+1	+2	ADD ON POINTS FOR
Finding it difficult to stay within the allotted time for your presentation						Planning and rehearsing your presentation so that you finish it on time
Reading the presentation from your notes						Speaking fluently without notes
Avoiding eye contact with the audience						Making eye contact comfortably with individual members of the audience
Sitting down to speak when the occasion demands standing						Standing up to speak and moving about
Only using text-based slides						Varying the content of slides to include text, pictures, charts and numerical data
Waffling						Being succinct
Being po-faced						Injecting humour
Sticking to your usual way of dressing regardless of the audience						Dressing to enhance the message of your presentation

Wanting to get the presentation over with as soon as possible				Managing your nerves
Not researching audience concerns				Preparing an audience profile
Ignoring the audience				Involving the audience
Keeping the volume, pace and pitch of your voice the same throughout your presentation				Varying the volume, pace and pitch of your voice throughout your presentation
Anything else				Anything else
total −2s				total +2s
total −1s				total +1s
total −1s and −2s				total +1s and +2s
Your **SNOOZE FACTOR** total score is:				

Take 2 points off if the observation on the left is **almost always** true for you.

Take 1 point off if the observation on the left is **occasionally** true for you.

Add 1 point if the observation on the right is **sometimes** true for you.

Add 2 points if the observation on the right is **almost always** true for you.

Add up your −2 and −1 scores for the left-hand column.

Add up your +2 and +1 scores for the right-hand column.

Subtract the left-hand column score from the right-hand column score. The resulting score is your personal **SNOOZE FACTOR**.

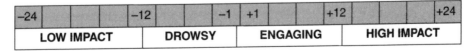

−24			−12			−1	+1			+12			+24
LOW IMPACT				**DROWSY**				**ENGAGING**			**HIGH IMPACT**		

TOP TO TOE CHECKLIST	
Hair brushed, combed, fluffed out, sleeked down	
Apply lipstick or lip gloss	
No lipstick or spinach on teeth	
Take the shine off your noise or forehead with tissue or pressed powder	
Check shoulders for dandruff, stray hairs (Sellotape is useful for quick removal	
Collar sitting inside jacket	
Buttons all done up, buttons in the right buttonholes (yes, really!)	
Knot in your tie is straight	
Bra is not showing	
Personal jewellery round neck is hidden	
Shirt tucked in all the way round at waist	
Check nail varnish for chips	
Belt buckle is centred	
Pockets are free of keys, loose change, wodges of tissues	
Trouser fly is done up	
Pocket flaps both in or both out	
Skirt not tucked into knickers	
Skirt lining or slip not showing at hem	
Tights free from ladders and snags	
Shoes and buckles done up	
How am I doing?	